Alexa:

999 Tips and Tricks How to Use Your Personal Assistant to the Fullest

(Amazon Echo Show, Amazon Echo Look, Amazon Echo Dot and Amazon Echo)

Alexa Richardson

CONTENTS

Thank you very much for getting this book!

We always try to give more value then you expect. That's why we've updated the content and you can get it for FREE. You can get the digital version for free because you bought the print version.

The book is under the match program from Amazon. You can find how to do this using next URL: https:// www.amazon.com/gp/digital/ep-landing-page

I hope that you will really enjoy reading it. At the end of the book, you will get a free bonus.

Introduction

When Amazon launched its Echo device and the corresponding Alexa voice control system in 2014, it brought hands-free technology into the home of the general consumer. In the years since Alexa has continued to be the most popular voice-activation software. It is expected to make up around 70% of the market in 2017 and is continuing to evolve with new offerings and features.

Alexa is an example of machine learning in action. It uses a smart artificial intelligence program to learn from the commands it's given, making it better and more useful the more you interact with it. This technology represents a drastic shift in how we as humans interact with machines.

With the Skills API that lets anyone create their own commands for Alexa, it's also able to evolve at the whim of the market more effectively than any other smart technology.

When it comes to developments for Alexa, 2017 is an especially exciting year. Amazon released two new Alexa-enabled devices to their product line: The Echo Show and The Echo Look. Whereas past Echos only used microphones and speakers, these new products also have cameras, meaning Alexa can see you as well as hear you.

All of the Alexa-enabled devices are linked to an app that you can either download on your phone or view online (alexa.amazon.com). This is where you'll see a record of all the commands that you've given Alexa and can customize the settings of the device to suit your lifestyle. The app works best with Amazon Fire tablets but can be accessed on any device.

If you've never experienced Alexa and want to get a sense of what using it is like, you can go to Echosim.io to scope it out without an Echo or other devices. This page will let you test out voice commands and play around a bit with Alexa's capabilities, so you know whether buying a device is the right choice for you. Of course, now that you can get an Echo Dot for as cheap as $30, bringing Alexa into your home is an extremely affordable option.

The information in this book is designed to introduce you to all the ways Alexa can help you to manage your schedule and organize your life. For many users, she's the perfect personal assistant, always ready to answer your questions and carry out your commands.

The additions of the Look and Show to the Echo line make

Alexa even more valuable. Using the camera on the Look, you can use the device as a personal stylist, helping you to organize your closet, plan your wardrobe, and choose the clothes that make you look your best.

Amazon has also added a new feature to Alexa in anticipation of the release of the Show, Alexa Calling, which is its own version of a FaceTime or Skype application. This gives you hands-free calling to anyone who has installed the Alexa app, along with some features not included in similar applications.

Whether you're considering your first foray into the world of Alexa or just bought a new device and want to find out everything it has to offer, the information in this book will tell you everything you need to know about Alexa's capabilities as a personal assistant—and just how helpful she can be in your life.

1 Chapter – Your Personal Voice Assistant

The voice control functionality of Alexa is extremely similar to using Siri on a smartphone. If you haven't used this kind of device before, it can be initially somewhat jarring, but it's extremely easy to learn the basics. Alexa is always on to respond to your queries and commands whenever you're in your home; the more you use the service, the more acquainted you'll become with what kinds of questions it can answer, as well as the array of helpful functions it can perform.

Alexa debuted on the Amazon Echo, a wireless cylindrical speaker that can also function as a smart home hub. Since the release of the Echo in 2014, they've added several new devices that can communicate with Alexa. The Amazon Echo Dot is a smaller, hockey puck-sized Echo designed for home use, while the Echo Tap is a portable version of the speaker.

Amazon also included limited Alexa functionality on all their FireTV products. These items range in price from around $30 for the Dot to around $180 for the full-sized echo.

All of the previous devices were focused on the microphone and speaker combination, but in 2017 Amazon took Alexa into the video realm. The Echo Look includes a camera along with the same audio performance as the Echo. The Echo Show takes it one step further, with a 7" display and a front-facing camera, for the first time letting Alexa show you pictures and videos. These devices cost a bit more (between $200 and $250) but are still extremely affordable, considering their functionality.

Regardless of which device you purchase, the first-time set-up is easy, even if this is your first time utilizing smart devices. When you take it out of the box and turn it on, the device will walk you through the set-up process.

Once this is done, you'll almost be ready to use your new device—all that's left to do is install the companion app on your smartphone. This app is completely free and works with both iOS and Android devices. It is where you can change any of the settings of your device, and also lets you see the command history or link your Alexa account to other services you'd like to use it for.

When you go into your app, you'll see a list of all the devices you have that can use Alexa. Be mindful when you change the settings if you have more than one device. Some changes will affect all of your devices, while others will apply only to one device or type of devices. It's a good idea to spend some time exploring the setting menu so you can get a better idea of your device's functions and features.

If you have a relatively small living space, Alexa can hear and respond to you from anywhere in your home. For larger spaces, Amazon offers a Voice Remote for $30. This can be paired with any Alexa device by going into the "Settings" menu on your Alexa app. Once paired, you can use it to communicate with your device, even if you're out of its hearing range.

Voice recognition

Alexa is a pretty smart piece of software, and it's capable of hearing and processing user commands straight out of the box. The program learns your voice the more you use it, however, and when you're setting up a brand new device you might find it's helpful to go through the Voice Training program so there are no misunderstandings while you and Alexa are still getting to know each other.

You can find Voice Training in the Alexa app. Go to the Menu, and then choose Settings, where you should see the Voice Training option. It can be a somewhat lengthy process, so make sure you set aside at least a half-hour before you start. You'll say around 25 phrases out loud when prompted. This will help Alexa to work with your accent and speech patterns more easily in the future.

Giving commands

Alexa knows that you're talking to it when it hears the wake word. By default this is "Alexa," but there are other options available. You can switch the wake word in the settings section of the app. After you say the wake word, you can ask questions and make requests in natural language.

There are a few commands you're likely to use frequently. At any point and in any skill you can say, "Alexa, stop," "Alexa, cancel," or "Alexa, help." This will interrupt whatever else is going on through your Echo. If you don't hear Alexa's response to a question, just say "Alexa, can you say that again?" and she'll repeat the last thing she said as many times as you need.

You don't have to be locked into a single phrasing or stilted way of speaking when you give commands to Alexa, one thing that makes it so much easier to use than many previous voice command products. If you want to change the volume, you can either say "turn it down" or "softer," and Alexa will understand you. You can alternatively give a numerical volume setting on a scale of 1-10, giving you lots of options. Not all commands will be as forgiving as this, but you won't have to do any linguistic contortions to make Alexa do what you want her to.

Location

Many of the most helpful features of Alexa—like giving you weather and traffic or ordering an Uber—can only be performed correctly if the device knows where you are. Because it's linked to your Amazon account, Alexa will already know your zip code, but you'll probably need to go into the Settings and manually enter your street address.

There's also the issue of a device's location within your home if you have multiple versions. Your device will be given a default name that's your first name followed by the product name (e.g. "Jill's Echo" or "Mark's FireStick") but this can get confusing if you have multiples of the same product. You can change the device's name under the Settings in the Alexa app. This way you'll know which one is in which room and be able to make changes accordingly.

Multiple users

Anyone who comes into your house can give Alexa orders just by saying her name, and you don't need to set up multiple user accounts to allow multiple people to use an Echo. If you want to be able to access the media libraries for multiple residents, however, you'll want to establish them as members of your household.

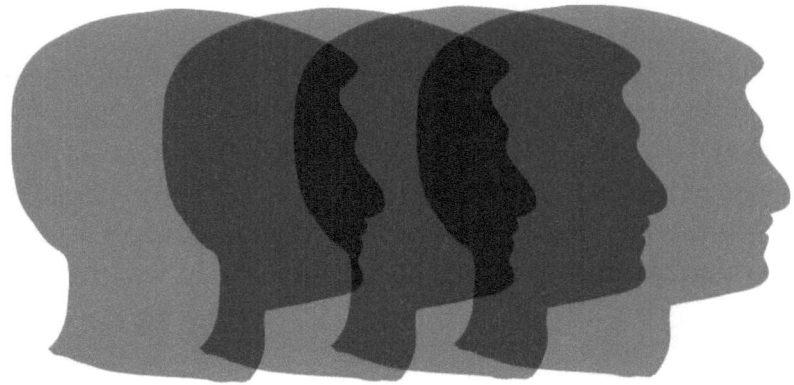

To do this, you have to go to your Amazon account page. Find the link that says "Household Profiles" and it will walk you through the process of adding someone to your household. You should have your house-mate with you when you do this, so they can enter any information the system needs when prompted. If you want to remove them later, you can do so at any time through this same page, though keep in mind they'll be unable to join another household for a period of six months.

Keep in mind that adding someone to your household affects more than the Echo's access to their library. It will also allow them to place orders through your Amazon account, give them access to some private areas of your account, and give their Amazon account many Prime benefits if you're a member and they're not. Make sure whoever you're adding is someone you trust with your personal information.

Separate user accounts on an Echo are somewhat limited. You can't add items to the calendars or to-do lists of household users, for example, or order things through their account. The main value, as stated above, is that it allows music, audiobooks, and other files to be accessed from the household account through any connected Alexa device.

If you have roommates or children, you may want to limit their ability to place orders on your Amazon account when you're not there. The easiest way to do this is to create a passcode for voice purchases. You can do this in the Alexa app, under the Voice Purchasing menu. There's also an option here to turn off voice purchasing if you want to avoid the situation entirely.

Alerts and alarms

If you find your alarm is too quiet, you can change the volume in the Sounds & Notifications menu of the Settings on the Alexa app. You can also change the sound that plays for an alarm, choosing from a variety of ring options and even celebrity soundbites to wake you up in the morning.

The Sounds & Notifications menu is also where you'll be able to toggle audio confirmation. In the default setting, you'll know Alexa has heard the wake word or has finished receiving your command because the ring on the top of the speaker will light up. If you keep the Echo or other devices in a place that's not easily seen, however, having it chime when it hears you can make sure you know when Alexa is listening.

Music and other audio

The Amazon Echo was labeled as a wireless speaker when it was released, and although its Alexa capability makes it so much more than just a speaker, it also makes a fantastic voice-controlled and hands-free option for listening to your favorite songs, audiobooks, and podcasts.

The default music player on Alexa is Amazon Prime music. This gives you a relatively limited library, especially if you tend to listen to more esoteric music. If you have an account with iHeartRadio, Spotify, or Pandora, you can link these to your Alexa account and use them as your default player, instead.

Go to the Menu, then Settings, and under your Account choose Music & Media. Scroll down to "Customize my music service preferences" and pick "Choose default music services," where you can select Spotify or another service as your main music player. The only major music subscription services that aren't currently compatible with Alexa are Google Play and iTunes/Apple Music.

You can also use your Echo or other Alexa-equipped speakers as a regular Bluetooth speaker, having them play music from another device or drive in your home. You can set this up by putting the device in Bluetooth pairing mode. At this point, you can say "Alexa, pair" and the Echo speaker will pair with your device. When you're done, just say "Alexa, disconnect" and everything will resort to normal.

Alexa also offers direct integration with TuneIn, which is a service that gives you access to an array of live radio stations and a large podcast library. You can have Alexa bring up the latest episode of a podcast just by saying its name. The only downside to this service is that it will only bring up the most recent episode easily with voice command. You can get to prior episodes by saying "Play the previous episode," but would have to do this over and over until you reached the one you were looking for. If you want to listen to a specific past episode, your Echo can still play it, you'll just need to select it manually by searching for it in the Alexa app.

Finally, if you like listening to audiobooks, Alexa can read those to you, too. You can link your Audible account directly to your account and then say, "Alexa, read the audiobook" and say the title of the book. If you don't have an audible account, you can also have Alexa read your books from your Kindle library. She can even pick up at the same spot where you left off the last time you were reading. Keep in mind, though, that if you have Alexa read your Kindle books she'll do so in her robotic voice, which some people find distracting, and which is certainly no substitute for professional narration.

2 Chapter – Setting Up

The whole idea behind the entire Alexa and Echo line is to be easily usable by anyone, no matter your level of technological experience and comfort. If you've never used an Echo device before, you might be surprised by how incredibly simple it is to set up. As far as the physical device is concerned, all you have to do is plug it in and it will start working for you right away.

You will also be required to download the Alexa app, which is free, to control the settings and features of your device. This can be installed on any smartphone that uses the Fire operating system, as well as any Android device (version 5.0 and higher) or any iOS device (version 9.0 and higher).

Alexa can also be used on any laptop or tablet. The newest generation of Fire HD tablets from Amazon come with Alexa capability installed. On other devices, you can simply navigate to https://alexa.amazon.com with any web browser. Its compatible with most common browsers, including Chrome, Firefox, Safari, and both Microsoft Edge and Microsoft Internet Explorer 10 or higher.

Once you've installed the app for Alexa and plugged in your Echo device, your set up is nearly complete—it really is that easy. There are a few other things you may want to think about, however, especially regarding specific smart devices and the arrangement of multiple Echo devices in your home. The sections that follow in this chapter will give you those additional set-up pointers.

Single Echo placement

The advanced technology used in the microphones on all iterations of the Echo has a surprisingly wide range. Even in a large room or with a lot of background noise you can count on the Echo to hear you and respond. The main thing you need to consider with the placement of a single Echo device is where you'll be most likely to utilize Alexa.

A kitchen or living room is often a great choice for general use. If you live in a small single-story space, like an apartment, you'll likely be able to make a request from anywhere provided you place your Echo in a central location. If you're outside of its listening area, you can also utilize Alexa through the app on your phone, though you'll need to press a button to activate it.

The strength of your Wi-Fi connection is also something to consider. Again, if your space is small, you likely won't have to worry about this much. If you have a larger space, however, make sure your Echo is positioned close enough to your Wi-Fi router that it can maintain a consistent signal. Keeping it away from any metal walls or appliances can also help to strengthen the signal.

Multiple Echo device placement

For most users, a single Echo won't be enough to bring Alexa connectivity to your entire home. The good news is that inexpensive options like the Echo Dot make it easy to put an Alexa-compatible device in every room, allow you to set up a truly immersive smart home.

Even more so than with a single Echo, making sure that all of your devices have a reliable Wi-Fi connection can be tricky. If your router and modem are centrally located and you have a wireless connection equipped to handle a higher number of devices, you shouldn't have an issue. In larger spaces, though, you may need to invest in a Wi-Fi extender, or even upgrade your wireless network to accommodate more devices.

The question of which Echo devices to put where is also one you'll need to consider. For many people, buying a pack of Echo Dots is the easiest way to outfit an entire home with Alexa. Many people find an Echo Show to be especially helpful in the kitchen. The Echo Look and Echo Spot are both designed for use in a bedroom, the first as a closet aid and the second as a bedside alarm clock. This doesn't mean you're restricted to these options, of course; any Echo can be adapted for use in pretty much any room of your home.

If you're using multiple Echo devices in your home, they'll use a system called ESP (for Echo Spatial Perception) to determine which device should respond to your commands. This eliminates the issue people often had before with the Echo's microphones hearing too well and having multiple Echos respond to your requests.

The ESP system is very good at telling which of your devices is physically the closest to you. The only downside of the system is that it can sometimes take a bit longer for Alexa to respond to requests, though the delay is negligible for most people.

Smart device set-up

The set-up process for each device you add to your smart home system will be slightly different, but there are a few general tips that you can keep in mind. Firstly, not every smart device will be able to interact with Alexa straight out of the box. Even if you have an Echo Plus with an included smart home hub, you will often need to enable an associated skill or set up an account through the device's brand before you can take full advantage of your options.

In many cases, enabling the skill associated with your smart device is all but automatic. You can simply say "Alexa, discover new devices" whenever you add a new one to your home. The Echo will scan for a few second then will add all the devices found right into the Alexa app, often enabling their associated skills at the same time.

If this process doesn't work, you have a few options. You can manually enable associated skill by going into the Alexa app and looking for the "Smart Home" section, then "Smart Home Skills." There are very few smart devices that have no Alexa compatibility at all. If you don't see a skill for your device, you may instead need to look for the appropriate recipe on IFTTT or Yonomi instead.

Finally, with all of your smart devices (including Echo devices), you'll likely want to re-name them within the Alexa app to make them easier to find. You can do this by going into the "Manage My Content & Devices" section of the app.

Keep in mind this will change the name for Alexa, but you may still need to go into the device itself and re-name it to make it consistent for Bluetooth devices.

Whatever you name your device is what you'll use to give commands, so you want to make sure you pick something that's unique, descriptive, and easy to remember. If you would like to use multiple names to refer to the same device, you can set this up using groups.

3 Chapter – Amazon Echo Look

The first thing you might wonder is what the Echo Look is, why you need it, and what's so great about it. Well, you're about to find out, for this chapter will discuss tips and tricks for this new device, along with just what in the world it is.

What is it?

So, what is the Echo Look? Well, it's a buildup on the original Echo system, and it adds a bit more assistance to your life.

Have you ever seen the movie Clueless? Where the girl asks for advice on how to pick out the perfect outfit? Well, the Echo Look basically does that, but it also comes with the features that are part of every single Echo system. Essentially, what you do is you take a photo, and this device will help you figure out recommendations, such as on outfits and such. You can even use this with the original Alexa features, such as the news, music, and home cooking appliance. How does this affect your life? Well, there are many different uses for it.

Alexa as your Stylist

With this device, Alexa now becomes your stylist and her main purpose is to make you look amazing. This Alexa device is intended to be in your bedroom or near your closet – whatever works best for you.

With Echo Look, allows you to take full-length photos of your daily, weekly or even hourly look by simply using your voice. The camera allows you to blur the background so that no one sees you surrounds and to enable your outfits to pop. In turn, it provides you with clean, ready to share photos.

The Echo Look provides the ability for users to get outfit recommendations for immediate use, a specific time frame, or even the next day. This feature allows you to plan your outfits in advance.

You also have the ability to Style Check to create a Look Book and even share your outfits with the world.

The Style Check team also wants to hear your feedback. If

there is a feature you think could be beneficial or is needed just drop their support team an email at support@stylechecked.com.

How it works

In order to get started with your outfit submissions, all you need to do is provide StyleCheck with a location and time when prompted. StyleCheck will then suggest an outfit that fits the weather.

New features are constantly being added to make your fashion life easier. You already stress about enough things, what to wear shouldn't be one of them.

So, what can Style Check do your you?

Benefits:

- Reduce stress and stay appropriately dressed for all occasions

- No more guessing, second-guessing and throwing clothes all over your room. Get some outfit certainty

- You will always be prepared for the weather. No more boots in the heat or shorts in the rain.

Style Check Features:

- Receive outfit suggestions for instant use, a specific time frame, or even the next day so you can plan your outfit in advance

- Receive outfit suggestions for any location

- Fast and easy to use. Get outfit recommendations in less than 1 minute

- For the techie, here is how Style Check helps you. Outfit recommendations based on the following technology:

- Uses Perez-Ineichen Solar Radiation models

- ASHRAE based thermal comfort model techniques

- Accurate Weather Data from http://Forecast.io

- Uses CLO (clothing thermal Insulation) ratings

In order for the Echo Look to be able to accurately judge visual information or your outfit, it needs a way to collect the visual information. The camera simply collects image or the light which has bounced off an object and records it using a sensor. Once this is complete, the information is then rendered in binary code, which is the computer's language of choice. Conversion to binary allows a computer to understand the information. The imagery is then assessed and judged.

It reduces a lot of stress that you might have when it comes to being dressed properly, and you can save a lot of time over the constant debates that you might have on what to wear. You can even skip the time frame if you want to, simply saying time frame when you're finished giving the location.

The echo Look also allows you to get a live view of your outfit with the Echo Look app. You can also use Alexa to take a short video so you can see yourself from every angle.

The camera and video functionality make it easier to get a full view of your outfit. The Echo Look's camera is enclosed by several small LED Lights which aim at providing you with a perfect, well-lit photo.

The camera is activated by simply using Alexa's wake word and adding the phrase "take a photo". When you say, "Alexa, take my photo", prepare to be captured. If you are looking to view your outfit in motion simply tell Alexa – "Alexa, take a video". After your image is taken the photos or videos are then uploaded to Amazon's cloud servers. The photos and videos are then sent to the associated smartphone application.

You can also take pictures of various objects, blue them out, and only have the focus on the object. You can use various skills enabled in order to ask Alexa to find information on this. Let's say that you see a strange animal on the ground, or maybe a bug got into your home that you have no idea what it is. Snap a picture, and then say "Alexa, ask Wikipedia what this animal is" and Alexa can do just that. It gives you a feel for what something is, and you can learn new information.

You can even use this with your selfies, and if you have Facebook or Instagram enabled, you can say "Alexa, upload this photo to Instagram with the caption __" and you can speak your captions. Alexa will do this for you in real-time, which is pretty awesome.

The Echo Look can be unintentionally aimed at the modern millennial. It is positioning itself as a fashion assistant. Once the Look takes a photo it will compare your outfits and make suggestions for various other fashion options.

You've finally gotten around to purchasing the Amazon Look, it's come in the mail and this is the moment you have been waiting for. You open the box and find the items listed below:

- The Amazon Echo Look device

  The Amazon Echo Look is Amazon's first device with a voice-activated camera. The device is white with a black face with white buttons. The Echo Look mimics the shape of an oversized pill — it is a cylinder with rounded ends. It sits on a stand or mounts to a wall

  The device also comes with a *white base with a silver leg.* The device has the ability to sit on a top of a desk or it can be mounted with the included wall mounting kit. This kit includes wall plates, screws, anchors, and instructions. The device also comes with the following:

- Power Adapter with a 7.9-foot cable.

- Quick start guide

- Things to try card

The Amazon Echo Look can be directly compared to the Amazon Echo. Although it is shaped differently and the Amazon Echo lacks the use of a front-facing camera, the 2 devices are quite similar.

Portable	No	No
Power	Power adapter	Power adapter
Wi-Fi	802.11a/b/g/n Dual-band (2.4 GHz and 5 GHz)	802.11a/b/g/n Dual-band, dual antenna (MIMO. 2.4 GHz and 5 GHz)
A l e x a Activation	Wake word Action button	Wake word
Camera	No	Yes
Buttons and Lights	Light Ring Action button Mute button	Front Light Ring Mic/Camera Off button Mic/Camera Off indicator
Bluetooth Audio Input	Yes	No

Bluetooth Audio Output	Yes	No
AUX Audio Input	No	No
AUX Audio Output	No	No
Compatible with Alexa Voice Remote	Yes	No
Accessories	Alexa Voice Remote*	Wall mount kit
Media Storage	No	Cloud
Alexa app	Yes	Yes
Echo Look app	No	Yes

Removing Stains now

Probably the coolest skill that you can get with this, is the removing stains skill. Have you ever just had a stain that you don't know how to get rid of, maybe on a blouse or something? Well, guess what? The Echo Look can totally help with this.

How does this work? It's simple really. Take a picture of the stain, and then say "Alexa, ask Good housekeeping how to remove ____ from ____" and from there you'll get a full set of steps on how to remove various stains from your clothing. You can even do this with upholstery or carpet, and also various garments as well.

Now, you need to, before you can even use this, make sure that you have Good housekeeping enabled on this. You can also use this skill with the Echo Show as well since it's got one of those front-facing cameras, and that is a good way to nip stains in the bud fast.

Now, you can use this with the other Echo systems as well, which is pretty great, and you can also enable a security camera function on this too if you want. But, probably the best feature of this, and the tips and tricks that do the best in terms of features are probably the ones related to your closet. The Echo Look is one of the best devices to create a hands-free photo or video, which is something that many like to have on hand.

Now, if you are worried about voice listening and photos being recorded, you can turn off listening and watching. If you do need this to be turned off, it will illuminate a blue light and you need to use whatever wake word you use in order to turn it on and let it listen once again. You can also cover the camera to make sure that nothing is recording it.

4 Chapter – The Echo Look & Your Privacy

With the advent of the Echo Look many people, rightfully so, have been concerned about the privacy of their video and face. The Echo Look essentially puts a camera in your bedroom. However, Amazon assures its users that their information is indeed safe. They do so by using the following security measures:

- Disallowing third-party application installation on the device

- Rigorous security reviews

- Encryption of images and communication between Echo Look, the Echo Look app, and Amazon servers.

- Amazon doesn't provide any personal information to advertisers or third-party sites that display Amazon's interest-based ads, according to the company.

If you still aren't completely sold on Amazon's security measures, there is a mute button on the side of the device which mutes the device and masks the camera. If that still isn't enough, unplug your device when it's not in use. Fortunately for you, your device remembers everything from the Amazon Alexa application and it will not hurt anything.

Ironically, everything that can be done with Amazon Look selfies, can already be done using the pictures that people have taken and posted online to a variety of social media sites. These pictures are not company specific and if warranted, anyone can get their hands on them. The only major difference between taking the cute selfies for Snapchat, Instagram and Facebook than with the Echo Look is that the Echo Look can give feedback on your "style" privately via the "Style Check" skill.

When you are seeking feedback on a specific outfit or photo this involves the image being backed up in the cloud, which can be done by Apple or Google and sending it out to social networks, messaging apps, text messaging or email.

Contrary to popular belief, taking pictures with a smartphone and sharing it online is still significantly insecure.

The Echo Look takes selfies to a new level, especially for beauty and fashion bloggers who now have the power to give their readers 360 outfit views. Not only are they able to get a full frontal and a 360 view – they are hands-free and can be taken simply with an Alexa command.

5 Chapter – The Echo Show

You might wonder just what the Echo Show can do. Well, you're about to find out, for this chapter will go over what the Echo Show is as a device, some of the cool things you can do with it, and some of the capabilities of the system.

About the Echo Show

The Echo Show is basically the Echo devices taken to the next level. This device will show you what you're looking for, and with the sound of your voice, you can control everything easily.

This system comes with a screen, a keyboard, and also some speakers in order to give you a crisp sound that is perfect for any room. It contains eight microphones noise cancellation, and even beam-forming technology. This system will react based on the commands even when music is playing.

In essence, this takes the Alexa system and enhances it completely. You can use this to call people, look up information, even read recipes to cook dinner. This device connects to Smart Home devices, and just from your voice alone, you control all of this.

Essentially, if you already have the Echo system, and you love it, you'll be able to take it a step further.

It's pretty light, being only about 41 ounces, about 7.4 inches high and 3.5 inches wide, so it's easy to carry around, and it even has dual-band Wi-Fi support. It all connects with the simple AC power chord that comes in there. The cable is about 6 feet long, so you can move it around.

It's quite an impressive system, and with Dolby stereo sound, it gives you the best that the Echo system has to offer, all in a simple package.

Why Would You Want This?

Are you someone that loves the Echo system? Then this is for you. With this system, it takes what the Echo had to offer, and gives you a screen.

If you loved your Echo device, but you don't like the idea of Alexa rattling off recipes in a confusing manner, or if you like visuals, this is perfect for you. The system comes with a screen, and you can connect to various sites to not only watch videos but to look up information, find recipes, and you can even get an accurate look at the weather and the traffic report.

Plus, the Echo Show helps connect your Smart Home devices in a much easier manner. With the screen, you'll be able to look at the various aspects of your devices, allowing you to control them. This system does support various music services, allows you to call others, and you can use this to do so much more.

This is perfect of those on the g, who don't like to sit at the office and look up information. If you're fine with talking to Alexa, who will help you find various information, then this is for you.

Control Everything with Your voice

Probably the coolest part about this is that you can control everything with your voice. It allows you to have a hands-free system for calling. You can ask Alexa to do virtually anything.

With this, you can get videos and messages between not only the Alexa app and your Echo Show, but also other Echo devices. You can talk to people with the Echo system or your app, and it's just that simple.

Not only that, there is the Drop In function, which allows you to check in on other rooms. If you, for example, put your kid to sleep and want to check in on them, rather than getting a baby monitor, you can have Alexa use Drop In to check that everything is all right.

With the voice feature, the future is now, and you can do all of this with the Alexa system.

The Echo Show is a great system that will allow you to expand your reach with these devices to new heights. You won't want to miss out on these features, and if you would like to control your entire home with just your voice, then this is the system for you.

Setting Up Your Echo Show

So, let's say you have the device, you're ready to get started with using this, but you don't know how to set it up. No worries, this chapter will take you step-by-step on how to set up your Echo Show so that you can use it in an efficient and rightful manner.

What Alexa Can Do

So, you've been hearing the name "Alexa" thrown around. What is it? What can it do? Well, you're about to find out.

Simply put, Alexa is a system that allows you to control your home and various devices with your voice. From music, to movies, to even asking what the weather and traffic will be, you can do all of this with the Alexa system. The Echo Show comes with a screen that shows you a picture, so that you can watch movies, play music, look up information, even use it to cook, and you can do all of this just with your voice.

Alexa is the system that you'll interact with when it comes to the Echo Show. We talked about what the Echo Show can do, but Alexa is really the one you'll be working with the most. It's a great voice control system, and you can even control your home via Smart Home devices. We'll go over that later on, but for now, let's get to setting up this great system.

How to Set up The Echo Show System

So how do you set up the Echo Show system? Well, it's a lot easier than you might think. You probably think it involves some sort of tedious connection, but that isn't the case. It's actually just a few simple steps.

First, you need to grab your phone, download the Alexa app, and then sign in. You can get this for various web browsers and smartphones, and this is where you essentially manage the Echo Show and the other options that you need.

This is available for the following systems: FireOS 3.0 or higher, iOS 9.0 or higher, or Android 5.0 or higher. You need one of these three to connect to this.

Now, you can download the Alexa app from either the Amazon Appstore, the Apple Store, or Google Play depending on what mobile device you choose to use. If you want to, you can also check out http://alexa.amazon.com if you want to do this on a Safari, Firefox, Chrome, Edge, or Internet Explorer 10 or higher if you don't have any of those devices.

Your next step, once it's all downloaded, is to then power up the Echo Show. Now, what's cool about this is that you can simply plug this into any power outlet that you have, so if you want to move it around, you can. You can then follow the prompts that are there to set it up, such as choosing language, Wi-Fi connection, synching your Amazon account, and reviewing the terms and conditions. Once that's all set up, you'll be able to then start using it.

Now you can then sync up your contacts and accounts and add all of that fun stuff into there. But, if you want to sync up your voice to Alexa, you need to say the "wake word" which is essentially the word that'll wake the system up. You can then speak normally to Alexa. Typically, you have to say "Alexa" to begin the system but you can change the wake word, which we'll discuss further in the next section.

And that's it! That's all you need to do to set up your device. It's that simple, and you'll be able to start using this right away.

Talking to Alexa

Now, talking to your Alexa device is pretty interactive, but you need to say a certain word first. For the Echo Show, you must say the wake word, and then the request.

Now the problem with the word "Alexa" might be the fact that your name is Alexa, or maybe you've got a family member named Alexa. What do you do then? Well, that's pretty simple. To change this, you first need to choose a wake word from the following: Alexa, Amazon, Echo, Computer. Lots of people like to use Amazon or Echo instead of Alexa.

From there, to change this, you go to Settings, choose the device, go to Wake Word, and from there you select the word and then save.

If you want to change the wake word on the device directly instead of via the app, let's say if your phone needs charging, you go to Settings, then Device Options, then Wake Word, and then choose your word.

How to Personalize Your Device

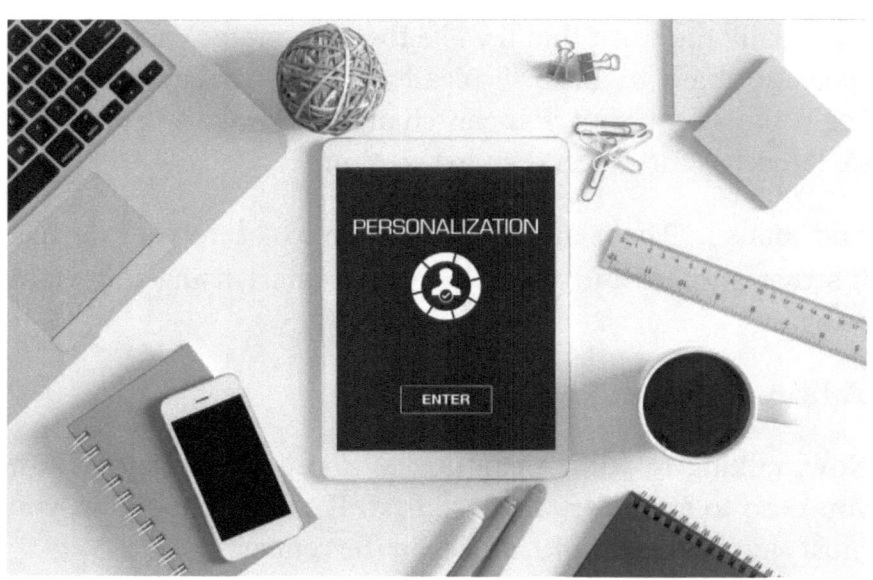

There are a few personal steps that you can take to really make your device your own. These are ideally done now, so that you can use the device immediately.

Now, if you move for example, and the address saved in Alexa is your old address, you can change this. To do so, go to Settings, choose your device, choose the Device Location, and then Edit. Once you fix the address, you can then choose Save. You can do this either on the device itself or on the Alexa app, Alexa also has a lot of skills. These skills can help not only connect your home devices, but also help you play games, check social media, or even tell you about upcoming events. How do you use this though? Well, it's that simple.

To do this, go to the app or say the word Skills. From there, you can then choose a specific skill, and once that's ready, you can open the page with the details, and then you can select the Enable Skill option. This is also how you connect third-party music and movie services such as Netflix, so keep that in mind.

You can even have Alexa put calendar events in. You can say "what's my next event" to find out what's next. You can say "add ___ to my calendar for (day) at (time)" in order to add events to this. If you already know of an event, you can say "add the event to my calendar. If you need to delete an event, you can choose it manually, or say "delete my (time) event" and it'll be deleted.

Finally, you can add traffic info to your Echo Show to give you an idea of what your commute will be like. To enable this, go to Settings, then Accounts and choose Traffic, and from there, put in the starting and ending point, and then choose Save changes to save the changes that you need to.

When it's time to get the traffic update, you can say "how's traffic," "what's my commute," or "what's traffic like right now" in order to get a feel for what you'll be facing in terms of traffic. The same goes for weather once you put in the device location and saying, "what's the weather" or "show me the weather" and you'll get to see it. You can also ask if it'll rain/snow/be hot or cold if you so want to, and you can check the weather in various cities. That's that simple but so very useful.

The Echo Show is an awesome device, and set up for it is pretty easy. Once you have it put together, you'll know what to do, and you'll be able to control your devices with your voice almost immediately.

6 Chapter – All About the Echo Spot, Echo Second Generation and the Echo Plus

Amazon is constantly rolling out new devices for you to try. They're varied in size and scope, and you might wonder what all of these do. Well, you're about to find out. This chapter will go over three new Echo devices: The Echo Spot, the Echo (second generation) and the Echo Plus and their capabilities that you can try out.

All About the Echo Spot

The Echo Spot is the perfect device if you want to put an Echo device in your bedroom. It's a device that has a small screen on it, and it's basically a smart alarm clock. It's kind of an enhanced Echo Dot or Echo Show, putting these two together in order to create a device that you can use around the house. It can be used as an alarm clock, but there are other uses for it, and it can be used in other areas of the home.

If you need an Echo device to make video calls, Bluetooth ability, music streaming, and other audio capabilities, this is a great device for it. It currently is heavily focused on music and streaming it, and if you want to play audio in various rooms, you can with this great device. It will be available starting December 2017, and it makes a great gift for the Echo lovers in your home.

The Echo Plus and other Neat Features

The Echo Plus is essentially an enhanced microphone system in comparison to other Echo devices. It does work as a smart home device, in that you can connect various gadgets to this relatively easily, but it has a super enhanced microphone field, and it also has a 360-degree sound along with Dolby sound. It has Alexa on there, and the Echo Plus is able to recognize more devices when searched. It also can connect more smart home items in order to hook them up to the Alexa system.

Now, another key part of this is that it does away with the apps and skills system that the other Echo devices had. In this one, it literally synchronizes everything by the cloud system, which is pretty wild if you think about it. It will synchronize everything locally in a room, so if for example, you wanted to hook up some lights, you can let the Echo Plus synch it, and it will hook it all up right then and there.

This, in essence, will make everything a smart home biome for you to work and live in, and while it's not just a speaker for Alexa that is enhanced, it also can connect to Samsung Smartthings, Apple, and Nest devices, which gives you a wider range of what your Echo device can hook up to.

The Second Generation Echo and it's Features

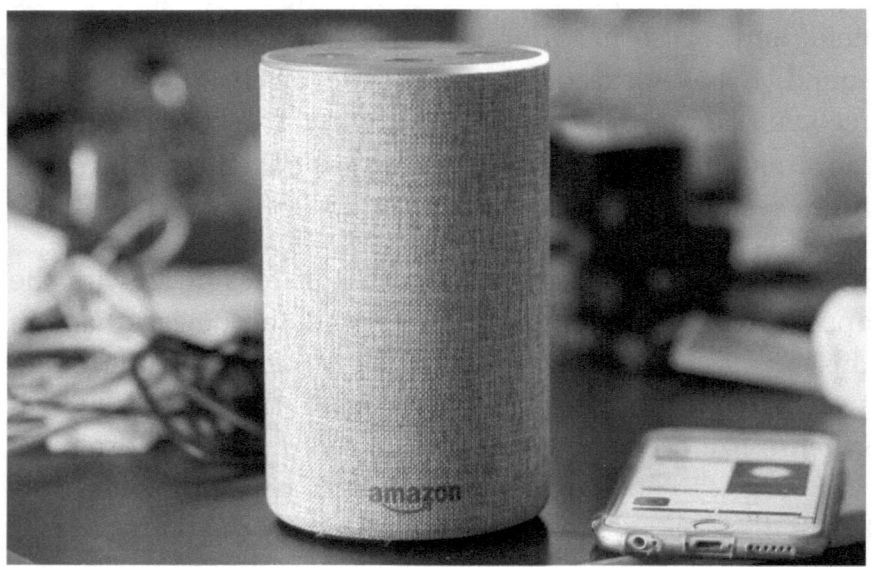

Finally, we have the second generation Echo, which in essence is a lot cheaper than the first generation systems. It is a much simpler design, with enhanced audio, and also a much cheaper price. Really, if you've been hesitant upon making this investment because you don't want to spend nearly 200 dollars on it, consider this one, since it's half the price of the other one, and it is much easier.

It is smaller, a more customizable face, and it isn't much different from the first generation of models. It does the same tasks as the other, can function using the wake word, and while the audio quality is still being improved, it might not be the best, but still does the job. It is definitely a decent system, however, and something to consider.

With this one, in particular, you might want to hold off if you already have a system. It doesn't have too many upgrades, so it might not be worth it unless you're trying to add more Echo devices to your home. But, if you don't have one already, and you want to take advantage of this system, it certainly does help, and it certainly can give you an enhanced smart home system. Plus, if you already have smart home devices, and you want to start using them right away, this is certainly a good place to go.

Ideally, you should from these three models, choose the one that best fits you. For many, the spot might be the one for you, especially if you're looking for a tinier device similar to the Echo Show, but you don't want to buy anything super bulky or the like. If you're looking for a means to hook up a lot of smart home devices all from the comfort of your home, and you don't want to have to manually put it all in, then you should consider the Echo Plus. But, if you're holding off on trying to get an Echo device, and now you're considering it, then this might be the best one for you.

All of these devices do work with other Echo systems, so keep that in mind. You can get the second generation, a couple of Echo Dots, or even a battery-powered Echo tap, and you can set all of these all around the room, use them, and see if that works for you. or, you can get one and have it somewhere, and use it around your home. Whatever it is, it's definitely a fun system to try out, and if you're considering going into the smart home mindset, it can be something worthwhile.

So, at the end of the day, these are a few devices that you can try out, based on hat your home needs. The Echo Show is probably one of the best on the market currently, but these new devices are all rolling out, and you can use them in conjunction with the Echo Show itself in order to create the best and most efficient smart home system that you can, and in turn, you'll make your life so much easier as well with these great devices.

Echo Dot

Amazon Echo Dot is designed to connect to an external speaker via Bluetooth or a wire. It supports voice interface and works with voice assistant Alexa. Echo Dot can reproduce streaming audio broadcasting, remind about upcoming events, report news and weather forecast, and also answer user questions by receiving information from the Internet.

ESP (Echo Spatial Perception) support allows you to use multiple Echo and Echo Dot devices in the same house, with the voice assistant Alexa responding to the user from the nearest speaker.

7 Chapter – Battery Saver Solutions on Echo Dots

Energy Saving

One thing that often becomes a problem for many Echo users, is saving battery. Sure, if it's plugged in, it does definitely do wonders, but if you're using an Echo Dot, chances are, you're running into the battery issue. What are some of the ways to best this though? Well, there are a few ways that can help you make the Echo Dot portable, and that's through the use of a portable battery.

Why make portable?

You might wonder why you want to make the Echo Dot portable. After all, it seems kind of silly, right? Well, if you're someone that doesn't have an outlet nearby and wants to playback music, order food, or even if you lose your phone or keys, this can be super helpful. If you're in a room that doesn't have an outlet, and you want to do this, it can help.

It's also good if you're creating a patio area and you want to do all of this. Setting up a couple of Echo Dots there while connected to another Echo system can give you everything that you need. You can even control the Google home and Siri-enabled gadgets, along with any smart home devices. You can make portable ones so that you don't have to go straight to your main Echo device.

How you do this, is to make it portable, and you do need a battery to make sure you can use it wirelessly. There are a few great batteries to choose from, so here they are.

Types of Batteries

There are two types that work best with the Echo Dot to make it portable, and these are either battery packs or backup batteries. You can also get the Tap as well, which requires simply tapping for it to work, but ideally, you should get an Echo Dot since you can do more.

A USB battery pack is also available as well, and this is a streamlined version of the other two options. It allows for more device compatibility, and it can be used with most devices so long as they're charged with a cable. You can go truly portable with the Echo Tap, but it's not really as good as the Echo, but there are some great portable batteries. If you're considering going portable, making sure that you have a Dot is really the best option.

There are a few great batteries to try out, and here they are below:

Fremo Evo: this is a battery that is intelligent, and it works with the second generation Echo Dots. It attaches simply to a magnet and doesn't affect performance as well. It's a high-quality battery that gives you a lot of juice, and for less than 20 bucks, it's worth the investment. It has about six hours of battery life, even in standby mode, which is the only downside to it, but it does allow for no interference, and it helps achieve the wireless Alexa experience.

Smarttree Battery base: this is a portable battery that is used for the second generation Echo Cot. This one has a stronger battery than the first one, and it allows for about 13 hours of use, so more than double what you're getting initially. It allows for a solid grip, and it does have a protective cover as well to shield it from elements.

Probably your biggest downfall to this one is the color, and the fact that it's only compatible with the second generation Echo Dot, so if you have the first gen, you're out of luck.

YutaoZ Battery Charging Base: this is a battery pack that works for the Echo Dot and the second generation one. Plus, it includes backward compatibility. Plus, you get some nice colors as well. You can use the USB port to charge any device as well, and it's kind of a universal battery pack. However, it is slightly cumbersome, because you need to attach the Dot to a sling tape. But, if you want to charge any USB-enabled device, it definitely can help with this. It's a universal charger, and it does good.

Now, it's versatile, and it has a good battery life, about 6 hours or so. But, if you don't like the tape, it might not be for you.

Poweradd slim battery pack: this is a portable USB charger that you can get that does offer more flexibility to your devices. It's compatible with the most USB enabled devices period. It's a great choice, in that's it's pocket-sized, charges fast, and you can see the charge level as well. It's cheap too, and you can get a GRDE version of this as well that offers more charge, solar charging, dual USBs and even a flashlight. This is probably the best portable charging option that you have, and it does the job well. It's not specifically for the Echo Dot, and the micro-USB cable is a bit short, but it definitely does work, and if you're trying to have a more portable experience with your Echo system.

These various Echo Dot chargers are solutions to giving your Echo Dot the portable life. If you've considered doing this in the past, but you didn't know how to, or really haven't explored the options of going portable yet, then this is definitely something to consider. There are many different benefits to this, a lot that you can get from it, and by exploring these, you'll be able to figure out what works best for you as well.

8 Chapter – Scheduling Your Devices on Your Echo Device

One thing that everyone wishes they could do with their Alexa device, is to schedule various activities to happen whenever you're trying to control devices in your smart home. Luckily, there are a few things that you can do, and this chapter will discuss how you can schedule your devices on your Echo device, and just how simple it really is.

Introducing Alexa to Wink

The first thing that you need to do is to create a Wink account, and from there, you'll connect Alexa to the Wink.

You'll first need to set up the account by first creating it, adding a hub to your Wink account, and from there, you can add the various bulbs, thermostats, sensors, and even locks that are controlled by smart home devices, and ones that do wonders. Now to introduce Alexa to this system, you want to go to the Echo app, and then go to settings. You go to connected devices, and under this section, there is an option called Link the Wink. From there, you will be asked to sign into the account that's associated with it, and then, you'll get access to it. Once it's confirmed, press the X button so that it's closed. You can from there press the Discover Devices option, and this will, in turn, read the settings of your Wink account, and learn about the connected devices. If you're worried she misses one, you'll be able to hear her say how many she's found, and at this point, you can then control the devices with a name.

That's simple, and if you want to schedule these, you can create an IFTT recipe for them as well. This is typically how it's done, and it does work wonders. It might be a bit complicated, but it is an option for those looking to learn more about the system itself.

Other Scheduling Options

There is another skill that you can enable that is called YONOMI. This is an app and a skill that has the capability to do this. It's a bit convoluted though, with the email server being a bit laggy in terms of when you'll be sending out messages.

In essence, it's simple. You go to the YONOMI app, and you choose the time and date for the event, and from there, set a location if that works for you. You then create the conditions that will make it valid. It doesn't command everything that Alexa can do, but if you set it up like this with a lot of the smart home devices, they do work. Currently, only about 90 items work with this system, but that's more than a lot of places, but if you do have the Hue lights, they work.

You then link up the app to your Alexa device, and from there, it will schedule it to come out in a certain time period. You can set up your devices, whether they're thermostats or even lights, and often, they work effortlessly. The only thing that you need to have for this, is your account email and passwords since this sets up just about everything. They're good one-time commands, especially if you want to schedule something, but if you want a recurring thing, it doesn't really do much good.

If you want to schedule devices, it does take a bit of work, but there are a few options that work well, and you can try them to see if they are fitting for you. It definitely enhances the Alexa environment.

9 Chapter – Calling and Messaging

The Alexa-to-Alexa calling service is another helpful feature for those who are looking for a complete smart home that comes installed on every Echo device. It's significant enough of a feature, though, that it deserves its own chapter. While this service is relatively new, Amazon has already made significant improvements to it over what was available when the service first launched.

The Alexa Calling service lets you make and receive calls between any Alexa-compatible devices. This includes Echo devices, Fire HD tablets, and any phone with the Alexa app installed. If both devices have a screen, it will default to a video call; otherwise, it will switch to a voice-only option. You can also send both text and voice messages to the same devices.

When you first set up the Alexa Calling and Messaging service, you'll be prompted to enter your cell phone number if it's not already on file with Amazon. This will sync your contacts from your phone with Alexa. If the person also has an Alexa account associated with their phone number, they'll be automatically added to your Alexa-to-Alexa calling list, as well.

Once you've completed the set-up, you can place a call to any number saved in your contacts simply by saying "Alexa, call" and the name as it's listed in your phone's contacts. If you're making the call through the app for Alexa, there is a second method of starting the call by clicking on the conversations tab (the speech bubble at the bottom of the screen) and search through your contacts there to place a call or send a message.

You can also call any phone in the United States, Canada, or Mexico by saying "Alexa, call" and reading the number. You will not be able to receive calls from mobile or landlines, however, unless they are connected to an Alexa-compatible device.

When you have an incoming call, the indicator light on your Echo will flash green and Alexa will tell you who's calling. If you're using device with a screen, like the Show or the Spot (or using the app on your phone) you will also see a contact card for the person calling. You have the option of saying either "Answer" or "Ignore" to any call that comes in. The indicator light will remain green for the entirety of your call. To end it, you can say either "hang up" or "end call."

If you miss a call or receive a message, the indicator light on your Echo will turn yellow, instead. You can use the command "Alexa, check my messages" to play any that are waiting. To send a voice message, use the command "Alexa, send a message to" and the name of the contact. Text messages can only be sent through the Alexa app, by clicking on the conversation tab in the bottom menu.

Preventing disruptions

Alexa has a mode that will keep people from disturbing you. Enabling it will do a few things. First, it will prevent any drop-in calls from coming in. It will also block alerts for incoming or missed calls and messages. It's different than muting the entire speaker because it will still allow alarms, timers, and notifications from other apps and programs to come through.

You can turn on this mode at any time by saying "Alexa, don't disturb me." When you're ready to turn it off, just say "Alexa, turn off" and the name of the mode. You can also schedule it to activate at a designated time by going into the Alexa app's settings, selecting your device, then looking for the appropriate sub-menu and flipping the toggle beside "Scheduled" to on. You can also change the start and end times by choosing the "Edit" option.

Setting up voice chats

Setting up voice chats is actually quite easy. To do so, you first need to download the Alexa app to your smartphone. From there, you can verify your mobile number and import the contacts to the Alexa app. Once Alexa has the contacts stored, you can then tell your friends about it if you desire, or just call them from the phone.

Now, to call someone, you need to sync your contacts to the app and then say "Alexa, call ____" and it'll do that.

If someone decides to call you, there will be a green light on your Echo Show. If you want to answer it say "Alexa, answer" and if you don't, say "Alexa, ignore" and it'll do that.

Echo Connect

This is one of Amazon's new line of "Alexa gadgets," peripheral devices that expand the functionality of Alexa. It expands the possibilities of the Alexa-to-Alexa calling system, incorporating your home phone in a way that can bring even this seemingly outdated technology in line with your other smart home systems.

Released in December of 2017, the Echo Connect is incredibly affordable at only $35. It plugs into your landline connection, and can communicate with any number of Echo devices, so long as they're all registered to the same Amazon account and connected to the same Wi-Fi network.

The Echo Connect lets you use voice control to call any number, even international numbers and emergency services that can't be called through the regular Alexa-to-Alexa service. There is no extra charge for this beyond what you pay through your phone provider, and the call will come through as your home phone line on the caller ID of the recipient.

Having an Echo Connect also means you'll be able to receive calls from any number, whether or not the person has an Echo device. Alexa will tell you when someone's calling, and will read you the name of the contact, as well, if that information is available.

Messaging with Alexa

If you want to message someone using the Alexa system, you can simply do so. This is a great function because you just need to tell Alexa to do it, say what you want to say, and it'll then send it.

For example, if you need to text your dad, say "Alexa, message dad" and then say your message. It's that simple.

If you have messages, then it might be best to check them right away. You can do so with the Echo Show as well. To do this, you first need to receive a message. You'll see a yellow light followed by a chime whenever you have one. You'll also be notified on the app in case you're not home to check it.

If you want to check your messages, say "Alexa, play my messages," or "Alexa, play ___'s messages" if you want it to just play a couple of messages from a certain person.

The best part about this is that you can use this with other Echo systems, and even with devices that aren't Echo systems. You can still call and message others if you want with this device. If you want to use this with people that don't have an Echo, can you still call or message from there. To do that, you need to make sure that they have the app downloaded so that calling and messaging is enabled.

With this system, you typically will use the calling and messaging function for everyone, and only use the Drop In function for those that you're close to, and to other Echos to check in on them. We'll go over what Drop In is later on.

The best part about this is that calling and messaging is free. You don't have to pay anything, just make sure you have a phone service provider with a verified number, and other people have the Alexa app downloaded.

The best position for recognition

One of the biggest things you might be concerned about is the placement of the Echo Show when it comes to calling. You want Alexa to pick up the calls and let you hear them, but you might wonder where you should put it. Thankfully, you're about to find out.

The ideal location for your Echo Show when it comes to calling it in the same room that you're in. That's because it'll allow for the least amount of interference, and this is a great way to hands-free call without having to blow out the speakers and such on your mobile device. You can take your Echo Show with you if you do want to move it to another room.

When it comes to the situation where you want to keep the

Echo Show in one place, but you want to still call from multiple locations, it's ideal that you put it in a space with the least amount of interference from electronic devices, and from walls. You should also make sure that Alexa can hear you, and you can test this by asking her something. If she responds, then you'll be able to make calls or have her message people. It's really up to you where you put it.

Ideally, keeping it in the living room so that you have access to it from other locations can be your best option. You can always test it by having others call, or make calls or ask Alexa to do other functions as well.

It's also a good idea to put this in your office as well, especially if you spend a lot of time in there and have a lot of video calls. You can ask Alexa to dial various numbers, and you can even see the person on the other end. That's the beauty of the Echo Show in comparison to other Echo systems. You can see the person, and do many other things as well, right from the comfort of your own home.

Calling is super simple with this device, and this chapter showed you just how to get started with this.

The Echo Show also contains another interesting feature called Drop In. Drop In is an interesting system that can be used not only to check on others, but it's even an intercom system. How do you use it though? Well, you're about to find out.

The Intent of Drop-In

The Drop-In system is a new piggyback system that's used for voice calling. This is actually intended to be used to call friends and family set up on the same system to check in on them. However, if you have multiple Echos or Echo Dots around the home, it can even be used as an intercom system.

For example, if you're cooking dinner and the kids are upstairs, or your husband is in the office and the food is ready, you can Drop In from the kitchen to the upstairs or office Echo, simply by using the Alexa app on the phone. It's pretty wild.

This is a system that lets you literally Drop In wherever you want to. The other person doesn't have to answer, and it connects you automatically to work like an intercom system in the house. You can speak and hear anything happen to the intercom system that you have it connected to.

If you use this via the Echo Show, you'll see the contact on the window once you connect to them.

How to Use It

To use it, you first need at least one Echo and one Alexa app that is installed and connected to the Echo. The Alexa app allows you to Drop In but you can't receive the call.

Now, to begin you need to make sure that you have the app up to date, and if you're not already subscribed to it, sign up for Alexa Calling and Messaging. Once that's done, open up the app, tap the conversations picture, which is basically the text bubble, follow the prompts, which is basically the caller information and number, and then it's all set up.

Now, you'll want to set it up to a specific speaker by pressing the Alexa app, tapping the hamburger picture, going to the settings function, and then choosing a speaker from the list. Make sure that when you go to the General setting, and make sure that it says On beneath the Drop In choice if you want calls from others. If you do want to restrict it, press Drop In and then touch Only My household.

To have Alexa Drop In on someone, you can simply say "Alexa, Drop In on ____" and the line is the contact name. You can manually do this by opening the app, going to Conversations, and from there choosing the conversation contact that allows you to Drop In and tap the Drop In that's located at the blue bar near the top.

You can also go to the Contacts tab in the right upper corner, press Drop In after choosing the contact, which is the icon beneath where their name is.

To use this as an intercom device, you first got to name the devices, you can then talk to Alexa and say, "Alexa Drop In on (room specified)" and then it'll Drop In on the room. You can manually do this too, but usually, Alexa works better.

Enabling contacts to Drop In

Now, this can be an invasion of privacy on many fronts, but Amazon won't just let anyone Drop In. It has to be from the contacts that you allow to Drop In on you, and you must have Drop In enabled on them.

To set this up, first, go to the Alexa app and press the tab called Conversations. Go to the contact icon, the one that looks like a person, and then choose a name from your contacts. You can then touch the toggle and choose Contact can Drop In any time. You can then check your contacts by going to the menu and choosing yourself. Then, check under what's called Others Who Can Drop In on My Devices and make sure that everyone who has permission is listed. You can press Remove if you don't want someone dropping in on you.

If you want to stop Drop In, press Do Not Disturb.

The Drop In function is a neat little addition that allows you to communicate with other areas of the home. Obviously, do consider the privacy aspect of this, and make sure it's not too invasive. However, it's still a pretty amazing system and one that can be used to help make communication a whole lot simpler.

10 Chapter – IFTTT

The acronym "IFTTT" stands for "If this, then that," and is a similar concept to the Alexa skills mentioned above. Like skills, IFTTT commands allow you to do more and control more devices with simple voice commands. Also like Skills, they're open for anyone to create.

Where IFTTT differs from the skills you can enable is in their ease of set-up. Whereas you have to be comfortable using the developer platform and doing some programming to create a skill, creating an IFTTT command is as easy as going to the website and following the simple onscreen prompts. Even home users with absolutely no experience with programming will be able to navigate these commands easily. Of course, you don't have to create your own commands if you don't want to. Just like with the skills, you can find a plethora of useful IFTTT recipes, known as applets, online for a variety of functions.

IFTTT is an online platform that allows you to easily connect and control devices and apps more intelligently. It is essentially a means of translating messages between devices so that you can allow one action (the "if then") to lead to another (the "then that") in a chain reaction. You can set up some fairly long and complex chains of commands using this platform, allowing you to greatly simplify the commands you say to Alexa to achieve a variety of tasks.

When you use them correctly, IFTTT applets are arguably the easiest way to completely customize your Alexa interactions, without having to wait for another user or a developer to create the action that you need. You can also tweak the applets available pre-made online, which can be a great way to grow accustomed to the process when you're just getting started.

There are a few limitations on the IFTTT system. First of all, it is currently only supported by devices in the United States or the United Kingdom; if you live in another country, you'll have to stick to skills. You can also only use IFTTT with devices and services that have set up a channel on the platform. Anyone with a product or service can inquire about creating a channel at any time, and the number of available channels is constantly growing—there were around 100 in July of 2014, but that number had grown to over 350 by the summer of 2017. Many of these channels come automatically pre-loaded with an array of applets specifically designed for Alexa to get you started.

There are a few smart home kits and products that don't have an IFTTT channel. If you want to be able to use these commands, search the IFTTT channel list before you purchase a new smart product to make sure it's supported. There are some surprising services that can be used in IFTTT recipes, as well, including online platforms like Twitter and

Instagram, along with personal devices like Fitbit.

You can loosely divide the channels available into three categories: online services (like Gmail or Bitly), hardware and devices (Google Glass or smart appliances), and functions (like weather or date functions). These channels can be connected into the same daisy-chain recipes; for example, you can use a date or time trigger to the power given devices on and off as well as send a notification to an online service.

While the concept behind IFTTT is simple, getting set up can be a bit trickier and time-consuming. You'll often have to download an app associated with the service if you haven't already in addition to enabling the channel. You also may need to create an account through the product or service's page. While all IFTTT channels are free to activate, some will only work if you've purchased the associated item or subscribed to a given service.

The more channels are added to IFTTT, the more useful the service gets. It can be used to make Alexa do all kinds of fun things. You can have it start your coffee brewing when a trigger from your fitbit tells Alexa you've woken up, for example, or have it turn your lights on and off at certain times while you're on vacation so it looks like someone's home. Once you have the basics of making recipes down and have the right channels, your possibilities are almost endless.

IFTTT recipes

There are three components to any IFTTT recipe: triggers, actions, and ingredients. The best way to differentiate them from each other is to use an example. Say you want your Christmas lights to turn on at sunset every night. The trigger in this example is the time that sunset occurs; the action is powering on, and the ingredients are the smart plugs your strands of lights are plugged into.

The way to chain applets together is to have the action of the first serve as the trigger of the second. You can do this as many times as you want. You can also tweak applets easily. If you decided you instead wanted the Christmas lights to come on when you said "Alexa, happy holidays," you could change the trigger to a voice command; the action and ingredients remain unaffected.

Every recipe starts with the phrase "ifthisthenthat" and builds from there. The online interface is very intuitive, walking you through each of the seven steps. If you mess up at any point along the way, you don't have to start over; just hit the back button until you get to the step you need to change.

The only limitation to the components you can use in the IFTTT are what kinds of things are available on the channel of the product or service you want to incorporate. Spend some time getting to know new channels as you enable them. Newer ones especially may be taking a gradual approach, which could mean that there aren't many actions available right now but there will be more in the future. Other services have certain limitations built-in, especially social media sites, which may seem silly to individual users but exist to prevent IFTTT from being used for spam.

Useful channels and applets

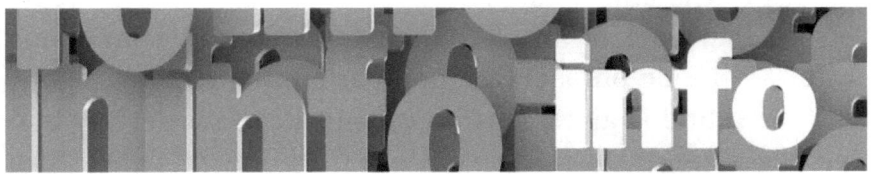

There are far too many channels to list all of them here, and with how often new ones are added, it would be outdated pretty quickly. Just like with skills, some of them will be fairly specialized or limited in their functionality, while others are must-haves for anyone with access to Alexa.

If you own any kind of smart device, you won't get the full value out of it unless you also enable its corresponding channel on IFTTT. Products that have an especially useful channel include Philips Hue bulbs and Nest devices, like their thermostat or Protect smoke alarm. If you want to use IFTTT with your home entertainment system, Harmony brand remotes allow you to stack your TV, audio equipment, and gaming console in a single device that has an impressive IFTTT channel.

There are some neat devices that are mostly used as an extension for IFTTT applets. One example of this is the Parrot Flower Power, a small device that you can insert into a flower pot or garden that will monitor the moisture and fertilizer content of the soil, as well as tracking the temperature and light levels. It's even smart enough to identify what kind of plant you have and what it needs to thrive. When the plant needs attention, you'll get an alert on your smartphone. If you've always wanted to have growing things in your home but have a historically black thumb, this just might be the perfect recipe for you.

Thanks to the ability to chain applets easily, you can create recipes that control all of the smart devices in your home with one simple phrase. One popular applet is "good night," which essentially gives your house a bedtime mode. Say that one phrase and you can have Alexa turn out the lights, turn off the TV, and adjust the temperature so it's ideal for sleeping.

Some of the coolest applets for the Philips Hue use the color options and dimming ability to excellent effect. You can have the lights brighten gradually when you wake up in the morning, giving you the effect of a natural sunrise and making the transition out of sleepless jarring. There's even an applet that makes the lights glow different colors depending on the weather outside, so there's no more wondering what to expect when you open your front door.

Some channels will give you unexpected side benefits. One example is WeMo smart plugs—another must-have channel for a smart home. By enabling it, you can not only use the plugs as ingredients in your recipes but can also use it to track energy usage so you can identify devices that are huge drains on your power. You can then set up an applet to automatically turn off appliances left running in the background, saving you money on your electricity bills.

The Nest Protect smoke detector is another smart device with an excellent IFTTT channel that every homeowner should check out if they haven't already done so. The applets provided on the channel can help you keep your home and family safe. You can get an alert when the battery needs replaced so you'll always know it's functioning correctly. It will also sense high levels of carbon monoxide and alert you if it's detected, then keep track of these instances so you can look for trends and prevent bigger problems.

Don't let this give you the assumption that IFTTT is only useful if you want to connect outside devices. It has a number of uses even if the only smart device in your home is an Echo. You can have it make your playlists into a Google Spreadsheet, for example, so easily keep track of which ones contain which songs, or share the info with people coming to a party so they can make requests.

Since you can use things like the weather, a date, or a time as the trigger, IFTTT is a great way to have Alexa tell you things without having to ask. Have it alert you when there's rain in the forecast so you don't forget your umbrella, or have it remind you of important dates like birthdays and anniversaries a few days ahead of time so they don't catch you by surprise.

Many online services also have very useful applets on their channel. If you're a sports fan, enabling the ESPN IFTTT channel will make it easier to keep track of your teams. You can set it up to automatically add their games to your calendar, and then send the final score to your phone once it's finished.

There are also many useful channels and applets that work

with your phone. The applet "find my phone" is one of the simplest and most popular. Just tell Alexa "find my phone" and she'll make it ring. If you have old iPhones laying around, you can use applets with those, as well. The Manything channel lets you turn them into closed circuit cameras. Just mount the phone or set it up on a stand and make sure it's on the same WiFi network as Alexa. Manything will use the camera to record video footage which you can then access remotely, checking on the daily report or reviewing footage from the last month.

Alexa does lists especially well. When it's time to take your shopping list with you to the store, you can search for it on the Alexa app, but for a lot of people accessing their e-mail is easier. There's a pre-made applet on the IFTTT site that will send your shopping list to your inbox on command. Just turn the applet on and give IFTTT access to your e-mail service. You'll be able to enter up to five e-mail addresses, so everyone in the household can have access to the info.

11 Chapter – Groups, Scenes, and Routines

Linking smart devices to Alexa through skills, IFTTT recipes, or Yonomi is a great first step to setting up your complete smart home, letting you add voice control to any number of appliances and functions in your home. As you accumulate a variety of different devices, though, you might find it a bit tedious having to give each command individually for each device.

This is where functions like scenes, groups, and routines come into play. Using these features can take your smart home set-up to the next level, letting you control multiple devices or trigger multiple actions and responses with a single voice command. Read on below for more information on the difference between these functions, and how to take advantage of them in your home.

Groups

Groups are a way to tie multiple devices together under one name so that you can control them all with a single command. For example, let's say you have three smart bulbs in your living room. Rather than telling Alexa to turn on each of these lights individually, if you create a group called "living room lights" you can control them all using a single voice command.

To create a group, go to the settings of your Alexa app and look for the "Smart Home" section, then tap "Groups" and select the option "Create group." You'll be prompted to give it a name; as with other names, make sure it's simple, descriptive, and easy to remember and say for commands. Next, you'll be asked to select the devices you want to include. You can add or remove items later on by going back into the "Groups" menu and editing the group in question.

You can create as many groups as you want to. There aren't any limits on how many devices you can put into any given group, either, so you can have groups with one device, or groups with dozens. Single-item groups can be helpful to expand Alexa's vocabulary, letting you essentially give two names to the same device to make it easier and more natural to use the voice control.

Scenes

Where you set up groups straight through the Alexa app, scenes are instead set up within the app of the smart devices you're using and then imported into Alexa after. They are most commonly seen in smart bulbs. Lifx color-changing bulbs, for example, give you the option of creating scenes to bring multiple bulbs to the same brightness and hue settings with one command; Philips Hue has a similar function.

Scenes are imported whenever you ask Alexa to discover new devices. Once you've imported the scene, you can activate it by giving the command "Alexa, turn on" and saying the name of the scene. Because they're set up through the app of the device itself, scenes are less useful at coordinating multiple types of device at once, but they can be helpful for making multiple changes to a set of the same device with one command.

Routines

Routines are a relatively new addition to Alexa's functionality, introduced only in November of 2017. They are very similar to scenes in that they let you trigger multiple actions with a single voice command, but also give you more options for controlling more devices than scenes are able to accomplish.

One great thing about routines is that you can combine smart home features with Alexa's weather, news, and traffic functions. Prior to the introduction of routines, your only way to do this was to daisy-chain IFTTT recipes together (more on that option in the next chapter). While routines are not yet as comprehensive in their possibilities as IFTTT recipes, it's a step in the right direction toward enabling these more in-depth controls directly through Alexa.

To create a routine, open the settings of your Alexa app and scroll down to the "Accounts" option. From this menu, choose "Routines" then tap the plus sign in the right corner to add a new routine. Tap "When this happens" to choose your trigger, which can either be a phrase or a certain time. If you choose a phrase, you'll be prompted to enter it; if you choose a time, you'll be prompted to select it.

Once you've added your trigger, you can set what you want it to do. Tap "Add action" and choose from your available options. You can pick as few or as many actions as you want. Once you've finished this section, you'll be asked to pick which of your Echo speakers the routine will run through. If you've chosen a trigger phrase, you can set it so that it's run through whichever speaker responds to your command.

If you want to change any aspect of your routine, you can do so by going back into the "Routines" section of the settings (following the same steps outlined above). You can then alter, add, or remove any aspect of the routine, then click "Save" to verify the changes.

As was mentioned above, the options with Alexa's routines are still slightly limited, especially compared to everything you're able to do using IFTTT. You can't use any third-party skills with routines, for example, and even on-board Alexa features like music playback and lists are unavailable. From a smart home perspective, though, they're a very useful way to simplify your Alexa interactions.

12 Chapter – How To Get Alexa To Play Movies And Videos

With the Echo Show, it gives you a chance to use Alexa to connect to various movie and streaming services. You can play videos on your Echo Show. How do you do this though? Well, you're about to find out.

Linking Streaming Sites to Alexa

With Alexa, you'll need to link the streaming services to this. It's pretty simple, but it'll allow you to access Netflix and other services.

To begin, you should first link the service to Alexa. You'll need to initially open the Alexa app, choose the app that needs to be linked, add in the login information, or create a new one, and from there, follow the on-screen prompts in order to complete this.

Now, let's take Hulu for example. You can choose Hulu, add in your account details, and from there, Alexa will allow you to stream this.

To do so, you can have Alexa open up Netflix by saying "Alexa, open up Netflix" and it will. From there, you can choose the movie, or if you know what you want, say it to Alexa. Say "Alexa, play ____" and Alexa will play the video that you want to watch. Streaming has never been easier, and you'll be able to use this with Alexa and the Echo Show efficiently.

Choosing an Amazon Video on Echo Show

To watch an Amazon video, it's basically the same thing. Amazon video is a free service for those that have Amazon Prime, and you'll be able to watch any of the eligible shows on this. You should first make sure Alexa is connected to this through the Echo Show, and then from there, you'll be able to use the service.

Typically, you can do a voice search on everything, and Alexa will provide you with what you need. For example, if you want to look for a video from your library, or maybe something you've had on your watch list, you can say "show me the video library" or say, "show me the watch list." Alexa will give you a full list, and you can go from there.

If you have a title in mind, you can say to Alexa "Alexa, show me ____" for the title of the show. If you don't get a response, sometimes searching via the name of the TV series works. If you want to watch Game of Thrones, for example, you say "Alexa, search for Game of Thrones" and it'll pop up.

Now, if you want to look for an actor or genre. Maybe you really want to watch that new Johnny Depp movie, but you can't remember the name of it, you can say "Alexa, show me Johnny Depp movies." And she'll do so. If you're just browsing online and you're looking in a certain genre, you can simply say "Alexa, show me (genre)" and she'll give you movies based in that genre.

You can even control what movie you want to say, and season of a show, simply by saying "Watch ____" or "Watch (tv series name) season (number)" and you'll get Alexa to play that. You can tell it to skip ahead by saying "Alexa, go back (x seconds/minutes/hours)" and you can do the same by saying "Alexa skip ahead x (seconds/minutes/hours." Alexa can do all of this and so much more, and you can tell it as well to go to the next episode too.

Watching movies and shows is so simple with the Echo Show, for it will give you the information immediately just by talking to it.

Watching YouTube on the Echo Show

Another app that many like to watch is YouTube on the Echo Show. With this, you can ask it to play virtually any sort of video. For example, if you want to watch videos of puppies, say "Alexa, show my puppy videos on YouTube." You'll get a full list of the various puppy videos that are available, and once you choose one, you can say "play" "pause" and "rewind" when watching this. After you've chosen the selected video, the Echo Show will even give you other options if you want to watch more. So, in essence, you won't stop watching the dog videos unless you say to do so.

Now, if you want to play the search results, you can say "play dog videos on YouTube." From there, the Echo Show will find the first dog video, and then it'll continue to play them all the way through the queue, which is pretty awesome.

You can also use the voice control for playback options that are in the video. You can first tap the screen to find these options, and from there, use them whenever you're navigating through videos. Playing videos on YouTube has never been easier with the Echo Show, and pairing it with Alexa gives you a whole range of skills.

One of the problems with the recent updates is that they pull YouTube from the Alexa system. Luckily, you can actually put it back on there, and you can do that through the Alexa Tube skill. This is available on GitHub, and it's a skill that will allow you to look for videos on YouTube to play with audio. You get about 15-18 hours of this per month, but you can also play these without audio.

The Echo Show is a great way to play various movies and

videos, and with the screen that it has, you'll be able to see the great content that you can watch easily, and control it all from your voice.

13 Chapter – Alexa's Most Helpful Features

While previous Echo models don't have the camera and video features of the new Look and Show, they still come with a plethora of options that make them extremely handy as digital personal assistants. One of the broadest ways Alexa can be used as a hands-free way to access the wealth of information on the internet. Most questions you pose to Alexa will result in a concise verbal response, and as the program learns while you use it, she'll be able to give you ever more accurate responses to your queries.

The seven microphones on the Echo use a specialized beam

technology to isolate your voice from the other sounds that might be going on in the house. Because of this, it has an impressively wide range, likely wider than you might expect. Unless you have an especially large house, Alexa will be able to hear you from pretty much every room—probably even beyond the range where you can hear her response. The video and camera features of the Look and Show are the only ones that aren't unidirectional, and can't be used as effectively from multiple rooms at once.

But those screens, as was mentioned in their chapters, give you a lot of benefits of their own. You can ask any Alexa device to check your schedule and tell you what's coming up on your calendar or ask it to add a new event at a given time. With an Echo Show, you can see those events on your screen, making it much quicker and easier to track which upcoming days are your busiest, as opposed to having her read off every entry on the calendar.

Regardless of which device you have, linking Alexa to your Google Calendar is the most useful thing you can do to turn Alexa into your perfect digital personal assistant. You can do this by going to your Settings on the Alexa app, then going into Account and Calendar, where there's an easy option to link to Google.

The Alexa app is also where you can manage all of your shopping and to-do lists that you've asked Alexa to add items to. Again, the Show gives you some definite benefits for this skill, displaying your lists on the screen command so you don't have to go into the app, but regardless of which device you have you can check your lists at any time through the app on your phone, or have Alexa read the items to you for a hands-free option.

As with calendar entries, you can link various other to-do list and shopping list apps to your account and use your Echo to control these apps with your voice. This can give you an expanded range of list options over the onboard ones Alexa generates already, helping you to stay organized and get to all of your various events and activities on time.

Alarms, lists, and keeping track of your events are the most common uses for Alexa across the board. If you're in the middle of something and can't look up at the clock, you can have her give you the time, or tell her to set an alarm for a certain time so you know when it's time to go to work or take care of other tasks.

There are also some tasks that are equally useful but less flashy and so don't get talked about as much when people are touting the benefits of Alexa. The fact that she can function as a hands-free calculator is one of these. If you're balancing your checkbook, asking Alexa to confirm your math can make sure you're coming up with the right figures from your calculations.

These math skills are perhaps at their most useful in the kitchen. Alexa can quickly perform measurement conversions. If your recipe lists things in grams and the packaging is in ounces, that used to mean putting everything down to take out your phone and search for the conversion, or else simply guessing and hoping it turned out right. With an Echo or other Alexa-enabled devices, you can simply ask for the answer and you'll get it.

News briefings

If you ask Alexa "What's new?" she'll give you the run-down of the day's top headlines in a Flash Briefing. You can customize what news you get when you pose this question by going into the Settings on the Alexa app. Select Account, then Flash Briefing, and you'll see a wide array of sources that Alexa can reference when putting together your daily report.

Depending on your preferences, you can aim the news toward world events or focus on more local happenings. You can add in updates on the sports that you follow, get financial news, or even find out about the latest celebrity gossip. If the options that come with the app don't seem to have what you're looking for, there are plenty of Alexa skills that can supplement your options; check out the next chapter for more info on those.

Keep in mind that not all the news sources will come with audio. Alexa will read you the ones that are text-based, in her usual robotic tone, which some people find jarring. This is most likely to be a problem if you're asking her for updates on the stock market; her pronunciation of the symbols may be difficult to parse through.

Traffic

Once you've entered the street address for the compatible device (which you can go through the Settings on the app) Alexa will give you accurate and up to the minute accounts of current traffic conditions. You can also give her the address of your destination and she'll figure out the fastest route for you to take.

You can save time on that last step by storing the address of your most frequent destinations. Go to the app Settings, then Account, and finally Traffic. Enter your work address, for example, and you can simply ask, "Alexa, how long is the commute to work?" She'll tell you what to expect on your drive to the office.

Shopping

Alexa will automatically be linked to your Amazon account when you set it up, letting you order things through the site with voice commands. This option used to be limited to items you had previously purchased, but Amazon recently expanded the options to a whole host of Prime-eligible products.

There are limitations to what you can buy through Alexa. Currently, you can't use her to buy anything from the Pantry, or any Amazon Fresh or Amazon Now items. You also can't use Alexa to buy clothes, shoes, or jewelry. It's possible this limitation on fashion and accessories will lessen or go away entirely now that they've released the Look, but for now you'll still have to order your clothes on the actual site.

You can also use Alexa to order items from other companies, though it will take a bit more set-up. If the brand offers a Skill for Alexa, enabling it will let you link your account on that site to her voice order capabilities. Exactly what you can order will depend on the company and the Skill; check out the next chapter for more information on Skills.

Alexa and smart homes

It doesn't take a big budget to set up a smart home using Alexa. You can buy smart plugs for around $35-$40 that will plug into any standard outlet and can be used to power a wide range of devices. The smart plugs from WeMo and TP-Link work especially well with Alexa. You can use voice control to turn any device running through a smart plug on or off on command. This will let you use voice control on any light fixtures that plug into outlets without having to purchase smart bulbs.

HOME SMART

Of course, if you want to set up a more elaborate smart home system, Alexa will still function beautifully as a hub. Alexa is compatible with a wide range of smart devices, including Philips Hue bulbs, Nest Learning thermostats, and devices from Wink, SmartThings, and Insteon. You can even find many appliances that come equipped with smart technology, like the WeMo-enabled coffee maker. Which items you buy will depend on your lifestyle, your budget, and how elaborate you want to make your smart home system.

If you have multiple smart devices in your home, you can also put them into groups to more easily control them. This will allow you to turn all the lights in a given room on or off at once, for example; you could even set up a Skill for when you're away on vacation, turning the lights on or off occasionally so it looks like you're home.

Placement of your device

The question of where to put an Echo or an Echo Dot was not a particularly involved one. If you lived in an apartment or small home, you could put it anywhere and interact with Alexa equally well; even in a large home, you could buy a Voice Remote or portable Echo Tap and get the full range of her skills anywhere.

With the Look and Show, this question gets a bit more involved. With the Look, the most obvious choice of where to put it is your bedroom, since it's designed to work with the clothes in your closet. This might not make sense, however, if you want the Look to be your only Alexa device and your bedroom is on the second floor, or otherwise isolated, which would limit the value of Alexa's other skills in the rest of your house.

The display screen on the Show makes it the most difficult one to find a home for. The screen is designed to be viewed easily from seven feet away, meaning you can see it from across the room when you need to, but not necessarily from the next room over—especially if there are walls in the way. You'll be able to use the voice command functions of Alexa in any room, so your main consideration should be where the screen will prove the most helpful.

While you might be tempted to put your Echo Show in a living room or office because those are the places you spend the most time, you may instead want to put it in your kitchen. You're likely to be in this room a lot while you're getting ready in the morning, which means it's the perfect place for quickfire questions about the weather or traffic, and the screen can show you what everyone in the household has on their agenda for the day.

Alexa can also be a great help at dinner time, displaying recipes, checking cooking times, or setting timers that you can watch countdown on the screen. The kitchen is also the room where you're least likely to already have a screen for watching videos or looking at images (although more and more fridges are coming with this option).

You can also easily manage multiple Alexa-compatible devices on the app and with the variety of types of device that are soon to be available, getting more than one makes more sense than it did in the era of just the Echo. You could have a Show in the kitchen, a Look in your bedroom, a Dot for the office, and a Tap on-hand for taking out into the backyard— or whatever combination makes sense for your living space.

14 Chapter – Amazon Echo Easter Eggs

There are many different Amazon Echo Easter eggs out there, and we'll go over a few of the best ones here below. This chapter will go into the more advanced Easter eggs, and you can use these to better understand your Echo device.

Say Almost Anything

If you need anything answered by Alexa, and I mean anything, you can certainly ask it. If you do, however, ask Alexa to say anything sensitive, such as swear words, they will get bleeped out, which is kind of funny. It does enable you to ask for various factoids, and that is something that is pretty cool about the system and allows you to truly experience Alexa.

Nighttime Mode

One thing that can get frustrating with the Alexa system, is when you're trying to settle in for the night, you ask Alexa a question, and then bam, you get a super loud response. If you want Alexa to play some music, but turn off the lights, it can be frustrating, since it often needs to be stated in various ways to get Alexa to understand. Fortunately, there is a way to do it, but you need to create the formula for it.

Essentially, you want to go to the IFTTT site, and you want to work with the lights that you have. From there, program them with a recipe that says, "If it's __ then the lights should go out" with the blank being the time. You can then say, "if the lights are out then Alexa should play playlist __ at volume __" and Alexa can do that automatically if you enable this recipe. It does take a bit of tinkering to master this and to even put it in, but if you want to have a means to quiet Alexa down, you certainly can.

It's also advised that if you want Alexa to be quiet, to turn it to sleep mode. That's essentially the large button at the top, and it will silence Alexa, allowing you to let it sleep.

Adding SoundCloud to Alexa

Another neat skill that you can enable, is putting SoundCloud onto your Alexa device. However, you will need to create this skill. To do so, you need to go to the Alexa skills kit section, get started, and from there, choose to add a new skill. You will then put in the name and the invocation that is necessary for this skill. You can name it SoundCloud, but you don't publish the skill. You can enable the audio player function for it then. From there, you go to the interaction model tab. You will need to look up the Intent Schema and the Sample utterances, and you can put the contents straight into there. You can choose the sample utterances that work best for you and put them into there as well. It's a programming code, so it's best if you don't know how to create this you literally just Google it and find it.

From there you go to the configuration tab and you will then need to put in the skill information tab where the application ID is, and you can put the whole id on there. From there, you can request the Soundcloud id to have the right redirect URL. You'll need to enable the account linking feature to do this to get the skills. You'll then get the redirect URLS, and you want to put the one that's starting with http:// layla.amazon.com   and from there configure the proxy server.

Now, to request the SoundCloud Client ID is simple. Fill out the registration and from there, you'll get the URL and you simply plug it in. You can from here get the OaAuth proxy server, and then prepare the DynamoDB instance. Both of these are found in the necessary files, and you need to configure them to your private key and certificate. You should make sure that you replace the redirect URLs with the one that you're given. For the DynamoDB console, you essentially create a table, name it SoundCloud-session and add the user as the primary key. You need to select the type string. You will then need to find the ARN, and it will start with the following: arn: aws : dynamodb and you need to make sure you write this down.

From there you create the lambda function, and on this page, you configure the triggers. You then add the skills kit that you have and that will, in turn, invoke the lambda. You will then need to upload the files, and you'll put in the Soundcloud id, the Alexa skill id, the dynamodb region, and the sessions table. You can then put in the lambda function and role, and from there, create a custom one. You can name it SoundCloud-lambda-execution, and you'll want to edit the policy to allow these functions, adding in the number on the ARNm for the dynamodb table, and then allow this. It'll then let you create the function, and you can find the ARN for the lambda as well.

From this point, you test the skill, enable it, and you can open the skills section and go to your skills, and it'll then link your account.

Google Assistant

You can put the official Google assistant on here as well. It has the same facilities the Raspberry Pi version of this, but it is limited in a sense due to the platform that it's on. You can only use about 500 requests on this currently, and only with US English. It does support IFTT, local search, and most actions as long as the responses take less than 90 seconds and don't use the home app.

Currently, this is a beta version though of the Assistant API, so if it does get updated, it might stop working, so keep that in mind.

Currently, it doesn't support alarms, timers, locating your device, playing music or podcasts, linking accounts to third-party services, or multiple users. If you want to use any of these, you should ask Alexa directly.

However, it does support the shopping lists that you do have, you just need to enable the app called Google express to see them, or if you need to do it from outside the country you'll need to search for it and download it here. You can use some local services as well.

It's a newer skill that might have some use, and it's definitely something to consider if you're fine with paying for AWS.

Ask Google Alexa Skill

This is a skill that you can install on your Alexa device. If you have ever had that situation where you ask Alexa something, and she can't answer, and it annoys you, then try installing this onto your Alexa device. This is something that can be used to ask Alexa to literally Google anything that you want to know.

Why would you need this? because while Alex is constantly being updated, it doesn't know everything, and it's one of the best skills to install. You can Google answers from your device immediately. Currently, though, it's not in the skills store, because they have a competing device, but if you're savvy with the Amazon Web Kit, you should be able to install this for free.

Pathfinder Skill

Do you play Pathfinder? If you're someone that does like Pathfinder but needs to know the stats of something or even the spell, it can be a nightmare sifting through all of the various books that you might go through. Fortunately, there is a skill that you can enable, two of them actually, that will allow you to not only find the stats for an item, spell, or monster that you're playing in Pathfinder, but also any spells that you're looking for. They're called Stat Finder for Pathfinder, and Spell Finder for Pathfinder. If you do want to get these, you have to go to the skill store, and you can get it publicly on GitHub in order to install this. This is a great skill for those that do play Pathfinder, and hopefully, there is one coming out for other tabletop roleplaying games as well.

Controlling Chromecast

If you have Chromecast, you can use GitHub as well to set up a Chromecast skill for Alexa to control this. It can pause, play, play various movies and trailers, set the volume, and also can stop this too. You can do this on a local network to connect to Chromecast. While Alexa does run on the cloud, you need to have both of them.

These various Easter eggs are great if you're looking for some hidden features, and if you want to truly amp up your Alexa device, this is the way to do it. By enabling third party skills, you can get way more out of this, and it's bringing Alexa to the future.

15 Chapter – Weird Alexa Skills to enable

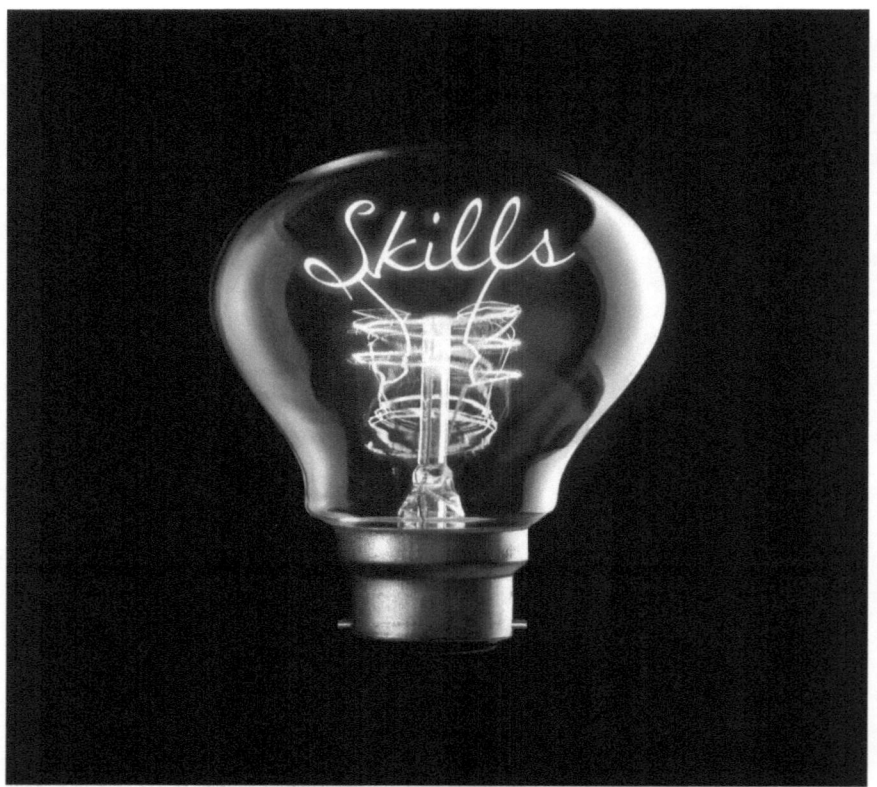

Now, you've heard of some of the normal Alexa skills, but what are some of the weird Alexa skills that you can enable, which might be helpful for you? Well, you're about to find out. This chapter will go over some of the weirdest Alexa skills out there, why they are weight, and why you might want to have these skills here.

Meow!

Are you a crazy cat person at heart? Do you like to confuse your pets like no other? Well, the skill Meow! is right for you.

In essence, enabling this skill will make your device sound like a cat. You can meow to this device, and it will make meows and purrs back. Maybe you miss having a cat near you, and this is a way to truly get that feeling back.

Pig Latin Translator

Does anyone still speak pig Latin anymore? If you're someone that does, or maybe you've heard people saying it and you don't remember what it translates to? Well, you're in luck, because with the pig Latin translator skill, you can ask Alexa a phrase in pig Latin, and she'll tell you the translation back. This can be fun to try out if you're someone that still does use pig Latin, or maybe you want to just brush up on it because some people like to say it.

Chat Bot

This is a chat skill that you can post comments from a Slack channel whenever you want. If you want to post a phrase to some channel you can. If you use Slack, this might be a fun one, or it might be a sign that you have a problem since you're using Slack for this system.

Cheap Date Night Ideas for $5

Don't get paid until the weekend, but you want to take your girl out somewhere? Well, there are some great cheap date night ideas, you just have to go look for them. By enabling this skill, Alexa will be your date decider, in that you'll get the best in cheap date ideas, and you can try them out. Whether they're something you and your partner like is up to you, but it's a fun one to try out.

MySomm

Are you a wino? Do you love the idea of drinking a deep wine, but you don't know what to pair it with? Well, download this skill. You essentially get ideas on how to pair wine with various foods. To get the service for this, instead of saying MySomm, you ask for "Wine Gal" and you'll get the recommendations that you need right away.

eHarmony

Are you looking for someone special, but you don't want to spend time perusing websites to find dates? Well, why not try the eHarmony skill? Essentially, you needed to enable this skill, sign in, and you can then tell Alexa to open it, and you can browse this with the power of your voice. Not only that, if you have a device with a screen, you can look at the matches and see if that's the right person for you. It changes the online dating game in a whole different way.

Egg Facts

Do you like really weird facts? Maybe you're someone who wants to know about some of the strange tidbits that are out there, including dogs, lipsticks, apples, and Belfast. However, this is one that will tell you all about the different egg facts that are right there. If you are someone that wants to break the ice by stating weird facts about eggs, then this is for you. It might not be particularly useful, but it's a strange Alexa skill that does work.

4Fart

Are Farts funny right? Well, you can now play fart noises with your Alexa device. That's right, if you want to hear funny fart noises, you say "Alexa, ask 4 a fart" and Alexa will play a fart for you. It's varying levels of sound and states, so it might be a bit repugnant, but it's definitely not a dull app, and it can be fun for the family.

Cork Ornaments

Some people really like cork ornaments. If you're one of those people that do buy them a lot, and you want to get the latest news on these, you can enable the skill for this. It will give you the best deals each day, so if you're feeling the urge to spend a little bit of cash on an ornament, this is the way to do it.

The grand tour

If you're wondering about a skill that's related to Top Gear, this is the one. It's one of those skills that might be a bit strange, but if you do open it up, you hear the banter from them, and they sound like they have guns to their head. The content in this is mostly trivia and exclusive videos that showcase upcoming episodes, and if you're a fan of the show, it might be something that could be quite fun for you. But if you're not a Top Gear fan, this might be kind of silly.

Remember your keys

Are you someone that makes others angry because you forget your keys? Well, you can stop doing that now. Literally, enable this skill and ask Alexa to remember if you have your keys. If you do ask, Alexa will remind you. If you don't have them, it'll tell you to find them. The one thing that sucks about this is that it doesn't have a Bluetooth tracker enabled, so it might not be super useful. It's a random skill that might be helpful if you're trying to remember something, but ultimately might be a skill that you ditch.

Alexa has some weird skills, and this highlights a few of the strange skills that are out there. They might be perfect for you, and it definitely is something to consider if you're trying to expand your Alexa skillsets to other realms.

16 Chapter – Some more skills

Alexa's AI is designed to learn and change over time, and the arrays of Skills you can add to its arsenal are one way that you can control and customize how it learns. Skills expand the abilities of your Echo beyond even its impressive functions right out of the box; giving you more commands to interact with more services—and even letting you create your own, if you're adventurous enough.

You can think of a Skill as an app for Alexa. Like an app, they can be developed by anyone, and must be manually added to your device before you can use them. There is a store you can access through the Alexa app on your phone where you can browse the available skills, similar to an app store. There are currently over 12,000 skills to choose from, and that number continues to grow. Thankfully, you can limit your search by category to help you find the skills you're looking for, or look up a specific skill by name.

Activating a skill is incredibly easy. Once you know the name of the skill you want to use, simply say "Alexa, enable" followed by the skill's name. You'll be able to use it instantly, with no delay in downloading or installation.

Once installed, the skill will have an invocation that lets you use it. This is similar to the wake word that activates Alexa. It directs Alexa to the right skill to carry out your task and can be the name of the company, the name of the skill, or some other easy to remember cue. As you activate more skills, you may find it helpful to keep a written record of each skill and its invocation, just in case you forget.

Because anyone can design a skill, some of them are more useful than others. Many are very specialized to work with a specific appliance or service; others are simply lacking in their functionality, or have issues that prevent them from working properly. If you're searching the skills on your own, you'll have to sift through a lot of options before you find the ones that will be useful for you.

To save you some trouble as you start looking through Alexa's skills, some of the most consistently useful ones have been identified here. They're divided into groups depending on their purpose. Certainly, they're not the only useful skills available for Alexa, but they'll give you a good starting point and an idea of what kinds of skills you'll find on offer.

Around the home

There are loads of skills you'll find you use every day to help you organize your life. Alexa comes with the ability to make to-do lists and add items to your calendar, and there are many skills that enhance these features. Quick Events makes it easier to set reminders and add events to your calendar.

If you're an iPhone user, you can send to-do list items you make with Alexa straight to your iPhone thanks to an applet made using the "If This, Then That" service. This is the same platform where you can set up your own command chains and sequences and is a useful one to get familiar with if you own a lot of devices that are smart-compatible but don't automatically hook up to Alexa.

Skills can also be used to further customize your daily news flash. The NPR Hourly News Summary skill gives you a 5-minute briefing on the day's headlines, updated every hour so you know you're always on top of current events. There are similar skills available from the Associated Press, as well as other major news outlets like CNN and BBC.

When it comes to getting financial news, Alexa skills in the past have fallen short, mostly because of problems with pronunciation of the various stock symbols. One that avoids this problem is Opening Bell, which lets you say the natural name of the company rather than its symbol, making it easier to get the information you need.

Alexa skills can also be helpful in case of emergency—both digital and physical. If there's a data breach on a site you frequent, you can check to see if your account's been compromised using the "Have I Been Pwned?" skill. It can be somewhat tedious in the execution since you'll have to spell out your entire username, but it will quickly bring up any security breaches connected to your name.

If you fall or have another emergency in your home that makes you unable to reach your phone, Alexa can come to your aid. Ask My Buddy is a skill that will send a notification to a pre-selected emergency contact by text, SMS, or phone call to let them know you're in trouble. It's no substitute for 911, but it could save your life if you're in a bind.

You can call on Alexa for more minor emergencies, as well— like, say, losing your phone. The TrackR skill can help you find it. You have to install the corresponding app on your phone first. Once you do that, enable the skill and you can ask Alexa to find the phone and give you the address. If it's nearby, you can have Alexa make the phone play a loud ringtone, even when it's on silent, helping you find it quickly.

Going out

Communication used to be one of the few areas that your Echo couldn't help you with. The Alexa Calling feature on the app and Show has changed that, but while that lets you make calls, it still doesn't send text messages. For that, you'll need the Molly skill, which lets you set up voice-controlled SMS in a few easy steps.

Start by registering at SMSWithMolly.com. Once you do that you can enable the skill and upload your contacts, giving them their own unique names. You can dictate your text to Alexa and she'll send it to the contact you designate—perfect for telling your friend you'll be a little late without interrupting your getting-ready routine.

If you're looking for a place nearby to go for dinner or drinks, you can enable the Yelp! The skill which can give you not only the names of local options but also their hours and phone number. You'll want to verify your address is entered correctly for the best results; you can do this in the Settings menu of your app.

The popular ride-sharing sites Lyft and Uber have skills for Alexa, as well. Once enabled, you can have Alexa order you a ride, check on how long it's going to take to arrive, or even cancel it if you change your mind and decide you'd rather stay in.

Finally, if your social call is of a romantic nature, you may want to consider adding the 1-800-Flowers skill to your device. You'll also need to have an account on the site to use it. Once your account's linked, you can use a voice command to order flowers and have them delivered to any address.

Entertaining

Alexa's onboard features already make it a great benefit in the kitchen, whether that's setting a timer or alarm to tell you when the cookies are done baking or asking it for measurement conversions and potential substitutes during the course of preparing the recipe. With the addition of a few skills, though, Alexa can become an entertainment powerhouse, guaranteed to make your next dinner party or friendly gathering a roaring success.

When it comes to cooking, there are arrays of recipe apps that you can enable that will help you find and prepare delicious meals. Best Recipes gives you the option to look up recipes based on up to three ingredients then has the option of narrowing the results depending on what meal you're preparing. The Campbell's Kitchen skill gives you give new recipe options every day that you can have sent to the Alexa app so you can prepare them. There are also apps from AllRecipes and several celebrity chefs. If you have an Amazon Show, these functions become even more useful, since you'll be able to display the recipe right on the screen.

Many appliances will also come with Alexa skills that let you use voice control. A lot of the current appliances that offer this ability are on the higher end of the price scale and are somewhat specialized and gourmet in nature, like the Joule sous, vie machine or the Anova Precision Cooker. The number of appliances that offer this kind of voice control connectivity is likely to expand in the future, however, and if an appliance is set up for smart control and Bluetooth or WiFi compatible, you can easily create your own skill to control it using the Alexa API.

If you'd rather order food than prepare it yourself, there are skills for that, too. Both Domino's and Pizza Hut offer skills that let you use voice activation to order your pizza. Other restaurants that offer delivery as an option are bound to follow suit as Alexa's popularity continues to grow.

Of course, a good party isn't just about what you eat—it's also about what you drink with it. There are a few apps to help you with this. MySomm is a skill that will help you to pair wine with food. It has hundreds of recommendations of what wines pair well with a range of ingredients. If you'd rather go the beer route, Check out the "What beer?" app, which will give you the same information but for beer instead of wine.

If your guests are more of the mixed drink crowd, check out the skill The Bartender. It has a library of over 12,000 cocktail recipes that it can recite to you on command. This speech-based answer can be a bit much to hear all at once if you're still learning how to make the drinks in question. The screen on the Show might help this out a bit, but in the meantime, it's a great way to refresh on the ingredients or order of a drink you're not quite sure how to make correctly.

Music is another key aspect of any party. The Echo's incredible voice command capabilities when it comes to playing music have already been discussed earlier in the book, but you can also find an array of skills that can interact with a broader range of music subscription services, as well as helping you to set up customized playlists and other helpful entertainment features.

Skills for travel

While you might think about Alexa more for its applications in your home, there are some skills you can get for it that make it helpful for planning travel, too. Perhaps the most useful skill is the one for the travel site Kayak. You can't use voice command to book a trip, but you can use Alexa to help you look up the lowest fare prices so you can get the best price when you are ready to buy your tickets.

There are also some helpful skills related to the airport. If you have people coming in from out of town, you can use the Landing Times skill to find out whether a given flight is on time or delayed. It can track flights from all the major airlines, including American, Delta, United, Southwest, Air Canada, Alaska, Frontier, and Spirit.

If you're the one taking the trip, using the Airport Security Line Wait Times skill can tell you what kind of delays you should expect in the security line. It gives you real-time data from over 450 airports around the United States and can help you make sure you show up with enough time to make your flight.

17 Chapter – Helpful advices

It can be tricky to use Alexa to her fullest extent when you're first getting used to how she works. How to phrase your commands to get the results you're looking for is the biggest hurdle for newest users? Compared to previous voice control systems, she understands natural speaking patterns extremely well, but she can have a bit of trouble with certain voices or accents.

If you're getting a lot of frustrating "fail" messages, your first step should be to go through the voice training described in chapter 1. This will make sure that the problem isn't Alexa's ability to understand what you're saying.

If that still doesn't seem to fix the problem, you may need to investigate just which commands she recognizes. The website CNET has a list of every single Alexa command available and updates it regularly to accommodate changes to the software. If you want to see commands specific to a device or service, you can also find those easily with a quick online search. Take some time when you add a new device, skill, or IFTTT applet to research the associated commands. You may find this also clues you into functions you didn't realize it had.

If you're having trouble with a skill, make sure you're using the right invocation. Because skills are created by outside users or companies, they are not always as intuitive as the functions that come with Alexa. Similarly, if you're using an applet, make sure you've got the right trigger, and that what you're trying to accomplish is actually supported by the channel.

Alexa constantly learns from the commands you give her, but if you want to speed up the process you can also guide her along by providing feedback. A card will pop up in the Echo app every time you ask Alexa a question or tell her to do something. You can use this to tell Amazon whether or not Alexa heard you right, information that will then be used to help her hear you better the next time.

One general piece of advice if you're trying to deepen your knowledge of Alexa's capabilities is to think beyond the obvious uses of some of the most common functions. Many people don't know that you can ask Alexa for the time in other regions of the world than where you're living. If your friend is visiting Australia and you want to know if it's a good time there to call and chat, just ask Alexa; if the city is over the dateline, she'll tell you the date as well.

Alexa is also knowledgeable about upcoming holidays. Being able to quickly find out what day of the week Christmas falls on can help you to plan out your vacation time. You can also ask Alexa to tell you exactly how many days you have left to shop, or how many days there are between any two dates that you give her.

Once you've activated IFTTT channels and enabling skills connected to certain services and devices, you can also use Alexa's variety of voice commands within these, as well. Asking "Where's my stuff?" will not only let you check on the status of any orders you've made through Amazon, it will also let you ask about the status of a pizza you ordered from Domino's, or tell you how far away your Uber is.

Even if you've had your Echo for a while, there might be things you didn't realize it could do or haven't had a chance yet to explore. The tips that follow in this chapter cover a range of topics to help flesh out your knowledge of Alexa. The more you know about what she can do, the better you'll be able to use her to organize and simplify your life.

Software updates

Alexa exists in the cloud, which means it is always connected to the network and can be automatically updated on a continuing basis. Most of the time this happens seamlessly, but if your Wi-Fi network is spotty or otherwise temporarily interrupted you could miss an update from time to time.

If you hear of a new feature that's been released but it doesn't seem to be available on your device, you don't have to wait for the device to update again on its own. Forcing an update is easy. When you put your Echo on "Mute" so that it can't hear commands, it eventually gets bored and looks for ways to keep itself busy. This will include double checking for new updates and installing them if it finds any. This takes about 30 minutes to kick in, so it's best to do it when you won't need to use Alexa for a while, like while you're at work or when you're sleeping.

Naming functions

Earlier in the book we discussed how you can change the name of your device to make it easier to identify, an especially good idea if you have more than one Echo in your home. But you can also set names for many popular functions on Alexa. This can be helpful if you want to use them to do multiple things at once.

The timer is one example of this. You can assign each timer with a specific title, like "rice cooker" or "chicken." This lets you check on the status of a specific timer or cancel one-timer while leaving the others going. If you want to see the status of all your timers at once, you can do so from within the Alexa app. You can do the same thing with your alarms, too.

You can also create names for other smart devices in your home, or create "profiles" that include multiple devices under one title. This is especially useful for setting up IFTTT applets. You can set up a profile group for every switch and light in the living room, for example, letting you turn them on or off with one command. There's no limit to how many devices can be in one group, or to how many profile groups you have.

Getting privacy

Most of the concerns people have about Alexa and her associated devices have to do with exactly what the service keeps track of. Though she's always listening, she doesn't actively kick on and start recording what you say until you say the right wake word. The "always listening" part of that is both what makes her so incredibly useful and what makes some people uncomfortable.

If you want to make sure that Alexa isn't eavesdropping on your more personal moments, you can easily mute any Echo device. All of them come equipped with a "Mute" button that completely disables the microphone. You'll know it's been muted successfully because the ring around the top of the Echo will turn red.

As was mentioned earlier, the cameras on the new Look and Show take the question of privacy and security to a new level.

Both devices have a mute button just like the original Echo; pressing this button disables the camera along with the microphone. Unlike the microphones, the camera is unidirectional, which also means you can turn the device around or lay it down flat if it still bothers you to have the camera pointed your direction. If you have Alexa Calling, don't forget to put it in "Do Not Disturb" mode so none of your friends drop in on you unexpectedly.

Uploading music

There are a few different ways you can have Alexa play music that you own. If you've purchased it from Amazon, you can access it automatically through the player. You can also use the Bluetooth or Wi-Fi connection to stream music files stored on solid state drives in your home.

The Echo and associated devices don't come with any solid state memory, but you can upload your personal sound files directly to the Cloud. Just go to the Amazon Cloud Player site and you'll be able to upload and store up to 250 songs for free. This will let you tell Alexa to play them even though the app, letting you take your favorite songs everywhere without having to suck up the memory on your phone.

More music tips

Sometimes you'll hear a snippet of a song and get it stuck in your head. It can be infuriating trying to figure it out. This is a problem no more thanks to Alexa. You can ask her "Alexa, play the song that goes..." and sing the portion of the lyrics that you can remember. She's usually pretty good at getting a match, even if you don't know many of the lyrics.

If you just ask Alexa to play a song, she'll use whatever music service you have set as your default to do so. If you'd rather go through a different service, you'll have to specify this by including the phrase "on Spotify" (or whatever service you want to access) during your command.

If you want to keep a record of the songs you've played on the Echo, you can enable an applet through the IFTTT interface to do so. It will keep track of your play history and save it to a spreadsheet that you can review later. To go the other way and play a pre-made playlist on your Echo, you'll have to say a fairly specific command. Make sure you say the word "playlist" after you've said the name of the playlist; if it's not on your default music player, make sure you also tell her which service to find it on.

Decision-making aids

Getting a piece of software to generate a random number is a fairly basic programming exercise, so it's not surprising that Alexa can do it so much as it's not a tool most people would think about. If you want to choose the team leader in a game of Trivial Pursuit or determine who get to pick the pizza toppings, you could have everyone guess a number and announce the closest to Alexa the winner.

If the choice you're trying to make only has two options, you can ask Alexa to flip a coin; she can also roll a set of dice. There's even an applet that will let you use Alexa as a magic 8-ball, though you should probably refrain from shaking and flipping your Echo.

Easter eggs and games

The people who developed Alexa have a sense of humor, and they've worked a lot of fun Easter eggs into the program. If you're not familiar with this term, it refers to a hidden feature placed into a piece of software for the user to "discover." For many people, a lot of the fun with Easter eggs comes from stumbling on them by accident, but if you're not concerned about spoilers, you can find extensive lists of them online. Most of them are related to the geek community or well-known pop culture touchstones if you're trying to find them for yourself.

There are other ways Alexa can help you pass the time. She'll play word games with you; Word Master is a particularly fun one. There is also a slew of different quizzes that come pre-loaded with the software, on topics like state capitals or trivia questions about animals. You might even find you learn a few things while you're using Alexa to relieve your boredom. Other simple games that Alexa plays include Rock, Paper, Scissors and Tic Tac Toe.

If you've got more time on your hands, check out The Magic Door, a speech command-based choose your own adventure game with a variety of different stories to choose from.

Easter Eggs are things Alexa can say that are not formally documented anywhere. They are cute and funny phrases that various Alexa users have found. Alexa possesses hundreds of Easter Eggs within her always growing the brain. These amusing hidden phrases are triggered by asking just the right questions. The list of some of Alexa's Easter Eggs below has been compiled from LinkedIn.

The Easter Eggs are as follows:

1. Alexa, 70 factorial

2. Alexa, all grown-ups were once children...

3. Alexa, all your base belongs to us.

4. Alexa, All's well that ends well

5. Alexa, Am I hot?

6. Alexa, Are there UFOs?

7. Alexa, Are we alone in the universe?

8. Alexa, Are we in the Matrix?

9. Alexa, Are you a robot?

10. Alexa, Are you alive?

11. Alexa, are you connected to the Internet?

12. Alexa, Are you crazy?

13. Alexa, Are you female?

14. Alexa, Are you happy?

15. Alexa, Are you horny?

16. Alexa, Are you in love?

17. Alexa, are you lying?

18. Alexa, Are you my mommy?

19. Alexa, Are you okay?

20. Alexa, Are you real? (multiple)

21. Alexa, are you single?

22. Alexa, are you sky net?

23. Alexa, Are you smart?

24. Alexa, Are you stupid?

25. Alexa, Aren't you a little short for a Stormtrooper?

26. Alexa, beam me up.

27. Alexa, can I ask a question?

28. Alexa, can you give me some money? (ask twice)

29. Alexa, can you lie?

30. Alexa, can you pass the Turing test?

31. Alexa, can you smell that?

32. Alexa, Cheers!

33. Alexa, Daisy Daisy.

34. Alexa, define rock paper scissors lizard spock

35. Alexa, define supercalifragilisticexpialodocious.

36. Alexa, did you fart?

37. Alexa, did you get my email?

38. Alexa, Do a barrel

18 Chapter – Tips to Using Alexa to the Fullest

Now there are still a few Alexa secrets that you can try out for yourself. If you're a loner, or maybe you just want to learn more things, then this is perfect for you. This chapter will discuss how to use your Alexa skills to the fullest, and some of the crazy things that you can do with Alexa.

Making Drinks

If you're with friends or even alone and you want to mix up some of the various drinks that you have, there are a couple of skills that you can try out. Turn yourself into the bartender that you've wanted to be with these skills.

The first is The Bartender, which has 10,000 drink recipes, and you won't' get bored with it.

There is also the Ask Patron skill, where it will give you drinks, various margarita recipes, and also some trivia about the great alcohol. If you want to just learn how to make stuff on your own, this is how you do it.

Lock yourself in Your home

For some of us, it's best if we don't have distractions. Well now you can, and you can actually lock everyone away with your voice. You can use this as an Alexa skill, and if you have the smart lock, it's definitely something that you can try out, and it will help if you're trying to get something done but don't need distractions. Or if you just hate the world and don't want to be around people.

Therapy

That's right, Alexa can be a therapy. Well, to a degree it can. It obviously doesn't replace a shrink, but if you need to just complain about the idiots that you work with, or maybe you're sad or frustrated, you can tell Alexa your problems, and it'll come back with some semi-useful information. It's not super helpful information, but hey, sometimes that little extra boost could be what gets you through the day.

Let Alexa Be your concierge

If you actually want to venture out of the house, but you don't really know what to get, literally you can ask Alexa. If you need a plumber, dinner reservations, or whatever, you can ask Alexa. If you want to, you can enable skills, such as maybe ordering a pizza, but it's also integrated with the Yelp system, so if you want some recommendations, you'll get the top results that are related to it, and if you need more information, it'll pop up on the app, which is pretty great as well.

Beating Boredom

If you want to get out and go to a hometown event, you might struggle to find some events online. But, if you want Alexa to do it for you, enable StubHub, and from there, you'll be able to find concerts, sporting events, and so much more. You can enable this, and then ask Alexa what's happening this weekend via StubHub, and from there, you'll get the results that you want, and pretty fast too.

Reading Books for You

If you don't feel like sitting down and reading, you can enable a skill to get Alexa to read to you. You don't even need another person to say the words. You use text to speech with whatever Kindle book you're reading, and from here, you ask Alexa to read your Kindle book, or the book title itself. It'll sync up with what you have left, and if you pick it up later, you won't lose your place.

Car Checkups

If you don't want to worry about running out of gas, or maybe how many miles you've driven, or maybe when you need to check your oil, you can enable the Automatic skill on this. You do need to have a sensor put into your car so that you get the information that you need, and once it's linked, you can ask Alexa where your car is if you need gas, how much you have left, and even how many miles you've gone. It's useful info that can help you a whole lot if you're considering this.

Always Update

One thing that you need to consider, is that if you want to have the best Alexa device, you need to make sure that the features are always updated. They do update every night, but if you do want to auto-update, you press the top button for about ten seconds to put it to sleep, to make sure it gets updated. It's best if you do this during a time period where you're not actually using it, but if you do want to check, you can always ask Alexa about the new features. Once they're fully installed, you can do the same thing as well, to great results too.

Create a Security System

One thing that you can do, especially if you have a larger home that does need some sort of security enabled on it, is to use Alexa as a means to create a security camera system. To do this, you need to have the cameras that are smart home compatible installed on there. If they for some reason aren't compatible with Alexa, you might need to create an IFTT recipe. From there, right before bed, you can schedule Alexa to turn them on, or if you're leaving your home for the day, you can do the same. This is actually a great thing to have since if you do enable this sort of thing, it will allow you to create a security system that can be used to protect you, and let's face it, it's a lot cheaper than buying a whole complex security system. You just need the cameras that are compatible and an Alexa device.

There are so many things that you can do with your Alexa device, but the biggest thing that you should do to use Alexa to the fullest as well, to use it. The Alexa system is here for a reason, and there are many benefits to using it. If you're curious about all of the features, you always can. There are also other skills that you can enable in order to make sure that you get the most out of it. You can search through the Alexa skills store, see more of what they have to offer, and from there enable it. You'd be surprised at what this has to offer, and all of the various factors that you can do, and some of the other great things that you can put on this.

Security cameras

There didn't seem many points to integrating security cameras with Alexa when it was mainly used through the original Echo speaker. Now that there are screen-equipped options like the Echo Show and Echo Spot (and Alexa integration on devices like the Fire tablet), getting a security camera that works with Alexa makes a bit more sense.

Netgear Arlo was the first security cameras that offered Alexa integration. They're built for outdoor use and pretty affordable, as weather-durable cameras go, at just over two hundred dollars each. The **Ring Video Stick-Up Cam** is another option that works well with Alexa. Its main benefit is ease of use. Ring also has a line of smart doorbells that can integrate with the security camera for more efficient use.

You can also get indoor security cameras that work with Alexa. These can be useful to keep an eye on your home when you're on vacation, or if you want to keep an eye on the kids' playroom while you're making dinner. If you're looking for a third-party option, **Nest IQ** makes a great in-home camera with a sophisticated AI that can send you alerts when someone's in the home it doesn't recognize.

Amazon also released their own in-home security camera as part of their Alexa Gadgets series, the **Cloud Cam**. Like with most of their Echo products, it's an incredible value at just over a hundred dollars. It even comes with a speaker and microphone so you can use it like an intercom. It obviously integrates seamlessly with Alexa and uses the cloud to store recorded footage, up to 24 hours for free, in addition to letting you check in on the live feed.

Smart locks

The kinds of features that you get by installing a smart lock vary widely from company to company. Some allow you to lock or unlock the door from anywhere, while others will only respond to voice commands when you're within your home. Some of them also include helpful features like digital keys that can be temporarily issued to specific phones, which can be a handy way to leave a key for a pet sitter or house sitter.

If you're looking for direct Alexa integration, the **August Smart Lock** is your best choice. It is currently the only option that lets you use Alexa to both lock and unlock your door, and uses PIN code protection for added security. It costs right around $150, comparable to other options on the market.

Alarms

Because many people use third-party alarm companies to handle this part of their home security, there aren't very many options out there for independent smart alarm systems. The best option that connects to Alexa is the **Scout Alarm**. Its on-board Alexa commands include arming and disarming the system. You can also call for help with voice control in the case of an emergency.

19 Chapter – Best Smart Home Devices to add to your Home

Now there are a ton of smart home devices, but we should know the best Alexa enabled devices for you to use. This chapter will go over the best ones, why they're the best, and why you should consider them, regardless of your home.

Philips Hue: if you need lights, you should go with Philips Hue. This will allow them to turn on and off, and with the scenes command, you can control a group of lights to do the function. You can even group them together.

WeMo: this is a product line that contains security cameras, but there are mostly light switches in this brand. Currently, Alexa can only do switches, but if you do want to at some point get a security camera, there are options. The switches here can turn on and off with a simple command and are integral to the home that you have if you want to control switches and devices.

Nest: Nest learning thermostats are some of the best. They're stainless steel in many cases, and you can control the temperature with your voice alone, and you can even set it to a temperature that you specifically want, or just up and down. This is great if you want to control different areas of the room and make them hot or cold.

Logitech Harmony: universal remotes are super popular, and you can use Alexa and this skill to enable these same functions without a remote. If you have this, and it's connected to your TV, you can turn it on, launch various streaming service apps, change your channel, and even control various system as well that you want to. It's a great way to control your home all with just your voice.

Curb Energy: this is a device that you put on the circuit breaker panel that's in the garage, and ideally outside of the house. Why do you need this? Well, if you're looking to save money and energy, this is the best thing to have, since it will allow you to monitor not only the energy output, and make sure you're not wasting energy.

SmartHub: this is something that's essentially a Wi-Fi electrical outlet. You can control anything that's plugged in with it, from the curling iron to the coffeemaker. It's useful if you want to turn things on and off immediately, and it does work.

Sonos Speakers: these are speakers that can be put anywhere, and if you connect them to the Alexa system, they can play music for you. It's an alternative option to the Echo devices if you already have a fitting speaker, and it might be better than the speakers on the overall Alexa device.

Lutron wireless Dimmer bulbs: these are great if you're looking to dim the lights in a room, or help to lower them whenever you need it. They also can control an outdoor light too, especially if you don't have ones that are weatherproofed. It can be a helpful device.

Chamberlain Garage Door Opener: this is an obvious one, and you can control this from your Alexa device or smartphone app. This is helpful so that with your voice, you can open and close it.

Fitbit: finally, there is the Fitbit. If you want to track your overall health and wellness, you can connect this to Alexa, and get the skill, which will, in turn, get you the information that you need on how far you've walked your sleep, and it can even track exercises as well, which is useful as well.

All of these devices are integral smart home devices that can make your life easier. Connecting them to the Alexa system can honestly change your life, and it can make the idea of controlling your entire home with your voice, and voice alone, totally possible, and also encouraged too, which is pretty great. If you're looking to take your smart home to the next level, this is how you do it, and it's pretty simple as well.

20 Chapter – Other Smart Devices

It's not much of an exaggeration to say you can get pretty much anything in a smart version these days. If you're looking for more ways to extend your Alexa smart home, the options in this chapter are all easy to integrate. It's certainly not a comprehensive list, but it's a good place to start your search.

In your car

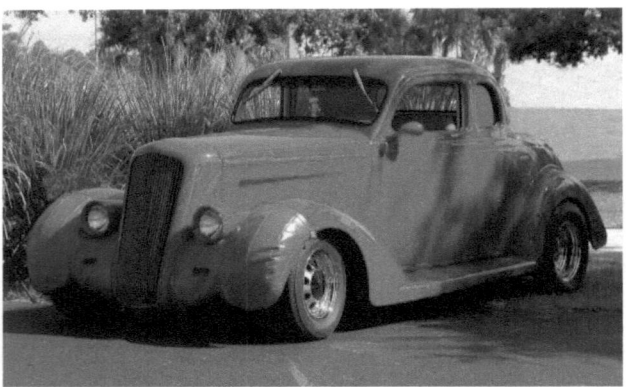

Believe it or not, you can now buy cars that come with Alexa integration built-in. The Ford Sync infotainment system has all the standard Alexa controls, along with some specific ones related to driving. Both BMW and MINI are also releasing vehicles in the next year that will come with Alexa already worked into the circuitry.

If you don't own one of these vehicles, you can buy a couple of devices that will accomplish basically the same thing. **Automatic** is a device that plugs straight into your car's diagnostic port and communicates with your smartphone via Bluetooth. It tracks your driving, fuel levels, and engine status, and you can also use it to help you figure out where you're parked.

Logitech also makes a product that integrates Alexa into your car, the **ZeroTouch Car Mount**. This means you can use voice control for things like navigation and playing music, letting you keep your eyes on the road.

In the kitchen

Small appliances have been coming out with smart versions for a few years. Mr. Coffee and Behmor both make coffee makers that are compatible with Alexa, and you can find everything from crock pots to sous vide machines that offer at least some smart functionality.

If you're shopping for large appliances, your options are more limited but also more impressive. LG has a few options, including the **LG Instaview Refrigerator**. The front door has a touchscreen and there are cameras inside, so you can browse the selections without opening the door—or even being in the room. GE is another company offering smart kitchen appliances. The **GE Profile Convection Range** has full Alexa compatibility, letting you check and set temperatures with voice commands.

In the yard

Alexa isn't limited to the inside of your home. You can find quite a few nifty smart devices that let you use your Echo to take care of your yard without leaving the house. **Rachio** was the first sprinkler system that could integrate with Alexa. Along with letting you turn your sprinklers on and off, you can create a schedule, set different sprinkler zones, and make quick adjustments from anywhere in response to sudden weather changes.

The **GreenIQ Smart Garden Hub is** another great option. It's more comprehensive than Rachio, designed to manage your entire yard and garden. You can link it up with your sprinklers as well as any plant sensors or weather stations you've got set up in your yard, and can even use it to control your outdoor lighting.

In the home theater

The easiest way to get Alexa on your TV is to use a Fire Stick or Fire TV Box. They've recently added the ability to pair Echo speakers with Fire TV devices for complete hands-free control of playback on Amazon Instant Video.

If you have a more extensive home theater set-up that you want to control with Alexa, consider buying the **Logitech Harmony Hub**. This lets you link your TV, gaming systems, and audio system into Alexa. Logitech equipment, in general, is a good way to go if you're looking to add smart capabilities to your home theater.

If you're in the market for new speakers, you could also opt for something from Sonos. Their Alexa skill has a wide array of features, and the **Sonos One** has the best sound of any speaker with built-in Alexa integration.

Conclusion

Amazon designed Alexa so that each user's experience with the program could be completely customized to their needs. The expansion of their device catalog with the new Look and Show only adds to your options, and almost anything you want to do with Alexa can be accomplished by enabling a Skill or using IFTTT.

The information included in this book is a basic overview of what you can do with Alexa, enough to get you started with using the device, but the truth is that Alexa is constantly evolving—one of the things that makes it so incredibly valuable. New Skills are constantly being added to expand Alexa's functionality. Since the program is completely Cloud-based, it is instantly updated and always being improved, often in direct response to consumer demands.

Being able to adjust your lights or heat with your voice used to be the stuff of science fiction. Even once it became possible, it was the exclusive domain of the wealthy, who could afford to set up elaborate smart home systems that had to be installed by professionals. This has changed again, however, and if you buy a $30 Echo Dot and a few smart plugs, you can set up a smart home for less than $200. Realizing just how affordable it can be often enough to make skeptics want to try it.

Now that you've gotten the basics of your device, don't be afraid to explore more options. The more popular Alexa becomes, the more companies are jumping on the bandwagon with their own smart versions of devices (and associated Alexa Skills). Even if you only use its basic onboard capabilities, getting familiar with Alexa will save you time and headaches, helping you to keep your life organized so that you can focus on the things you want to be doing.

I hope that you really enjoyed reading my book.

The free bonus will be waiting for you at this link
https://helpfulwriting.wixsite.com/bestauthor

Thanks for buying the book anyway!

For your notes -

If you already have Alexa-enabled device or just bought a new one and want to find out everything it has to offer, the information in this book will tell you everything you need to know about Alexa's capabilities as a personal assistant—and just how helpful she can be in your life.

Amazon designed Alexa so that each user's experience with the program could be completely customized to their needs. The expansion of their device catalogue with the new Look and Show only adds to your options, and almost anything you want to do with Alexa can be accomplished by enabling a Skill or using IFTTT.

The information in this book is designed to introduce you to all the ways Alexa can help you to manage your schedule and organize your life. For many users, she's the perfect personal assistant, always ready to answer your questions and carry out your commands.

Here is a preview of what you'll learn:

- Amazon Echo Style Check
- Voice Calls and the Drop in Function
- Alexa's Most Helpful Features
- IFTTT
- Helpful Tips